RECKONING OF POWER

Oppenheimer, the Atomic Bomb, and the Second World War

HISTORY BROUGHT ALIVE

RECKONING OF POWER

© **Copyright 2023 - All rights reserved.**

Published 2023 by History Brought Alive

The content contained within this book may not be reproduced, duplicated, or transmitted without direct written permission from the author or the publisher.

Under no circumstances will any blame or legal responsibility be held against the publisher, or author, for any damages, reparation, or monetary loss due to the information contained within this book, either directly or indirectly.

LEGAL NOTICE:

This book is copyright protected. It is only for personal use. You cannot amend, distribute, sell, use, quote, or paraphrase any part, or the content within this book, without the consent of the author or publisher.

DISCLAIMER NOTICE:

Please note the information contained within this document is for educational and entertainment purposes only. All effort has been executed to present accurate, up-to-date, reliable, complete information. No warranties of any kind are declared or implied. Readers acknowledge that the author is not engaged in the rendering of legal, financial, medical, or professional advice. The content within this book has been derived from various sources. Please consult a licensed professional before attempting any techniques outlined in this book.

By reading this document, the reader agrees that under no circumstances is the author responsible for any losses, direct or indirect, that are incurred as a result of the use of the information contained within this document, including, but not limited to, errors, omissions, or inaccuracies.

FREE BONUS FROM HBA: EBOOK BUNDLE

Greetings!

First of all, thank you for reading our books. As fellow passionate readers of History and Mythology, we aim to create the very best books for our readers.

Now, we invite you to join our VIP list. As a welcome gift, we offer the History & Mythology Ebook Bundle below for free. Plus you can be the first to receive new books and exclusives! Remember it's 100% free to join.

Simply scan the QR code to join.

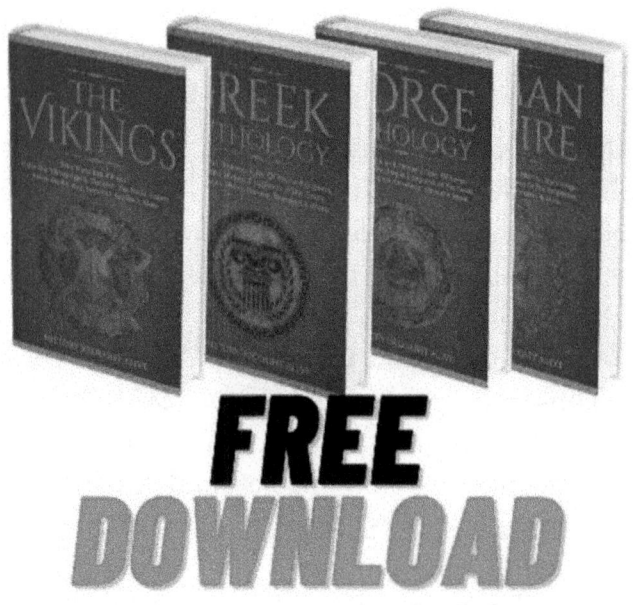

Keep up to date with us on:

YouTube: History Brought Alive

Facebook: History Brought Alive

www.historybroughtalive.com

CONTENTS

INTRODUCTION 1

CHAPTER 1: PRELUDE TO POWER.................. 7

    THE WORLD SET FREE 7
    $E = MC^2$ 10
    ENTER NIELS BOHR 12
    REALIZING NUCLEAR FISSION....................................... 16
    ENTER ENRICO FERMI.. 19

CHAPTER 2: WORLD AT WAR 23

    ANTISEMITISM AND THE NAZI ATOMIC PROJECT 23
    A LETTER TO THE PRESIDENT 29
    AN OVERSTATED FEAR 34

CHAPTER 3: THE MANHATTAN PROJECT'S GENESIS 37

    THE GENERAL 37
    THE FATHER OF THE ATOMIC BOMB 41
    PRACTICAL CONCERNS...46
    COMPARTMENTALIZATION AND SPYING........................52

CHAPTER 4: ARCHITECTS OF DESTINY 57

    AN EMBARRASSMENT OF RICHES 57
    THE DRAMA OF THEORETICAL PHYSICS 61
    THE CHICAGO METALLURGICAL LAB.............................64
    THE IMPLOSION DEVICE 66

CHAPTER 5: THE BRIGHT GLARE OF TRINITY 71

    THE PRELIMINARIES 71
    SOME CONCERNS... 75
    THE WORLD, FOREVER CHANGED 77
    CELEBRATION AND AWE 81

CHAPTER 6: ETHICAL CROSSROADS 85

- THE PACIFIC THEATER 85
- THE FRANCK REPORT 88
- OTHER MORAL QUALMS 94

CHAPTER 7: UNLEASHING THE BEAST 99

- LITTLE BOY AND FAT MAN 99
- THE SELECTION OF HIROSHIMA AND NAGASAKI 104
- THE IMMEDIATE IMPACT 106
- LONG-TERM CONSEQUENCES 110

CHAPTER 8: COLD WAR AND ARMS RACE ... 113

- STALIN AND TRUMAN 113
- THE DOWNFALL OF OPPENHEIMER 116
- THE ARMS RACE 125

CHAPTER 9: LEGACY AND LESSONS 129

- PUTTING THE GENIE BACK IN THE BOTTLE 129
- THE LEGACY OF RADIATION 134
- NUCLEAR WEAPONS AND INTERNATIONAL POLITICS ... 137
- EFFORTS AT DISARMAMENT 140

CHAPTER 10: NUCLEAR POWER AND FUTURE CHALLENGES 143

- NUCLEAR ENERGY 143
- THE CHERNOBYL AND FUKUSHIMA DISASTERS 146
- THE DREAM OF FUSION 149

CONCLUSION 153

REFERENCES 159

INTRODUCTION

"I have become death, destroyer of worlds."

This line from the *Bhagavad Gita*, a sacred Hindu text, is probably the most famous of J. Robert Oppenheimer's quotations. It encapsulates a sense of awe, an indication of ego, and, perhaps, a smattering of guilt. Like the man who quoted these words after seeing the world's first nuclear explosion, they are complex and full of subtext.

However, Oppenheimer did not say these words while at Trinity—the site of the atomic bomb test. He said them much later after two atomic bombs had been dropped on the Japanese cities of Hiroshima and Nagasaki. To all accounts, Oppenheimer was not somber after the successful Trinity test. He strutted about, enjoying the success, laughing and smiling with other members of the project. It is possible he was thinking those words of the *Bhagavad Gita* inwardly, but such sober considerations were hidden behind an exterior swagger.

At Trinity, the Manhattan Project had succeeded in creating a functional atomic weapon. Oppenheimer was the director of the project, a project that at its peak employed 130,000 men and women, and cost approximately $2.2 billion (equivalent to over $21 billion in today's money). An undertaking that in the normal course of science would have taken decades was achieved in three years. As President Harry S. Truman (1945) would later announce, after the bombing of Hiroshima: "We have spent two billion dollars on the greatest scientific gamble in history—and won."

As such, maybe we can forgive Oppenheimer's swagger. It may have been hiding all manner of emotions: guilt, awe, a sense of profound history. But, most of all, it was probably hiding overwhelming relief. The United States was the first country to build an atomic bomb, and all the money and trust invested in Oppenheimer's project was justified.

In this book, we chart the history from the

conception of the Manhattan Project to its culmination at Hiroshima and Nagasaki, and beyond into the Cold War and the present day. The beginning of the atomic age is a fascinating period of history, filled with fascinating characters, world war, tense geopolitics, and fraught politics within the United States. And then there is the bomb itself: a world-changing, revolutionary technology that may not have ended war, but forever changed it. The subject matter is rich with ethical complexity, and complex individuals who were forced to grapple with terrible moral decisions. Was it right to design the atomic bomb? Was it right to use it on Hiroshima and Nagasaki? Was it right then, to develop the hydrogen bomb? Have nuclear weapons made our world safer or more dangerous? These questions are as difficult to answer today as they were in the 1940s and 1950s.

However, with this period of history being so rich and complex, there is a danger of becoming lost among the weeds. If you are reading this book, you are presumably curious to learn more about the birth of the atomic age, but it can be difficult to keep track of every twist and turn across this challenging time of human history.

At History Brought Alive, we have found the

solution is to focus on a character-driven narrative style, in which our history follows the remarkable individuals at the center of the story. Throughout this book, we will consider some incredibly influential men, including Albert Einstein, J. Robert Oppenheimer, Edward Teller, General Leslie Richard Groves, Niels Bohr, and Leo Szilárd. Some of these men, like Leo Szilárd, had profound doubts about the morality of the atomic bomb project, and even greater doubts about the use of atomic bombs in war. Others were more enthusiastic about the project, such as Edward Teller, the father of the hydrogen bomb.

The focus on key figures helps make the scientific and historical events of this period both relatable and engaging. This book also delves into the sociopolitical context of the Second World War and the Cold War, exploring the motivations and decisions behind nuclear weapon development. We address ethical dilemmas, along with the long-term consequences of the bombings of Hiroshima and Nagasaki, encouraging critical reflection from you, the reader. We make extensive use of primary source material to offer diverse, first-hand perspectives of what it was like to live in this period of history, but we also discuss the legacy of the atomic bomb and its impact on global politics and nuclear power. This book also makes a sharp distinction between nuclear weapons and energy and discusses challenges and opportunities associated with nuclear technology: from fission to fusion.

Here at History Brought Alive, we are experts in history and mythology. We have sold tens of thousands of books on topics from Egyptian mythology for kids, to the history of modern Ukraine, and received many five-star reviews. We specialize in achieving what our name suggests: bringing history to life by focusing on character-driven narratives and providing first-hand accounts of fascinating periods of human history. In all of the books in our series, we ensure that key moments of human history—as well as vital parts of human mythology—are made accessible to the average reader, allowing readers of all backgrounds to understand the powers and stories that have shaped the modern world. This book, like any in our series, is suitable for anyone, whether they are already enthusiastic readers on the topic or readers who know practically nothing about what happened at Los Alamos under Oppenheimer's leadership of the Manhattan Project. At History Brought Alive, we welcome anyone with the curiosity to learn more about the history of the human world.

In focusing on the characters of the Manhattan Project, as well as the ethical implications of the development of the atomic bomb, we do not ask you to come to one conclusion over another. We are not here to present an argument and browbeat you into believing it. Instead, this book exists to inform and empower you, so that you can reflect for yourselves on the legacy of the atomic bomb and the responsible use of technology for a more peaceful future. You may find that some facts and considerations surprise you. If you come to the subject with certain pre-held beliefs, you might find that you change your mind. Either way, you will know more about the Manhattan Project, and be able to utilize our extensively researched and meticulously sourced work to reach your own conclusions.

With that in mind, we hope that you enjoy this book. Embark on an enlightening journey through the history of the Manhattan Project, and join the quest for knowledge and understanding—a quest that can shape a more informed and conscientious global dialogue on the profound impact of the atomic bomb.

CHAPTER 1
PRELUDE TO POWER

The World Set Free
Written in 1913 and published in 1914, the author H. G. Wells made a chilling prediction in his novel *The World Set Free*. Released just before the advent of the First World War, Wells predicted the use of atomic weapons:

Such was the crowning triumph of military science, the ultimate explosive that was to give the "decisive touch" to war... A recent historical writer has described the world of that time as one that "believed in established words and was invincibly blind to the obvious in things." Certainly, it seems now that nothing could have been more obvious to the people of the early twentieth century than the rapidity with which war was becoming impossible. And as certainly they did not see it. They did not see it until the atomic bombs burst in their fumbling hands. (Chapter 2, Sections 4 & 5)

It is unclear whether all or many of the key players in the Manhattan Project read *The World Set Free*, though it is known that both Winston Churchill and the Manhattan Project scientist Leo Szilárd read Wells's books. If other scientists on the project had read this book, they might have seen parallels to their own attitudes and naiveties. J. Robert Oppenheimer, Niels Bohr, Albert Einstein… were each ultimately wrapped up in their own world of academic collaboration and political idealism. They belonged to a community that "believed in established words and was invincibly blind to the obvious in things" (Wells, 1914), that shared research and findings regardless of nationality or creed. They were, in some ways, naive to the fundamental divisions between nations that would lead to two world wars and then a Cold War between the United States and Soviet Russia. We can only speculate how this informed their approach to the Manhattan Project, but this naivety and idealism is evident in their writings and conduct, from Oppenheimer's carelessness with security and left-wing activities to Einstein's urgings for a world government to manage atomic weapons.

In either case, Wells's book proved to be a remarkable prediction of events to come. Though a work of fiction, *The World Set Free* (1914) predicted the use of atomic weaponry and the moral horror that such bombs would inspire:

The catastrophe of the atomic bombs which shook men out of cities and businesses and economic relations shook them also out of their old established habits of thought, and out of the lightly held beliefs and prejudices that came down to them from the past. To borrow a word from the old-fashioned chemists, men were made nascent; they were released from old ties; for good or evil they were ready for new associations. The council carried them forward for good; perhaps if his bombs had reached their destination King Ferdinand Charles might have carried them back to an endless chain of evils. But his task would have been a harder one than the council's. The moral shock of the atomic bombs had been a profound one, and for a while the cunning side of the human animal was overpowered by its sincere realization of the vital necessity for reconstruction. (Chapter 4, Section 11)

$E = mc^2$

One of the most famous physicists to ever live, Albert Einstein, was born on March 14, 1879, in the German city of Ulm. His characteristic wild hair and absentminded nature would become a trope for brilliant scientists in movies and the rest of the media, from Doc Brown in *Back to the Future*, to Frederick Frankenstein in *Young Frankenstein*.

Einstein was a Jewish man. In February and March 1933, the Gestapo—the Nazi secret police—repeatedly raided his family home in Berlin and their family cottage, which was later turned into a Hitler Youth camp, and Einstein's sailboat was confiscated (Yachting.com, 2023). In April 1933, the Nazis passed laws that prevented Jewish people from holding any official positions at government institutions, which at this point included teaching at universities. As it was, Einstein had already seen where things were going. Harboring a deep disgust for the Nazi regime, Einstein had already renounced his German citizenship on March 28.

In May 1933, the Nazi book burnings began. Einstein's works were among those targeted for destruction. Later, Einstein would write to his friend Max Born (also a theoretical physicist), "I must confess that the degree of their brutality and cowardice came as something of a surprise" (quoted in Isaacson, 2007). By then, Einstein had emigrated to the United States, later becoming a United States citizen in 1940. Like many of the greatest scientists of his age, he refused to work for the fascists because of their racist and small-minded beliefs.

Einstein was already a famous physicist by the 1930s. In 1921, he won the Nobel Prize in Physics, after publishing his paper on the general theory of relativity in 1916. And, in 1905, he published four revolutionary papers in the field of theoretical physics in what was called his miraculous year. One of these papers, published in *Annalen der Physik*, would not only change physics but also the entire course of human history. In this paper, Einstein introduced the world to $E = mc^2$: the equation that started the atomic age.

The equation remains Einstein's most famous achievement. In $E = mc^2$, "E" stands for energy, "m" for mass, and "c" denotes the speed of light. The equation states that energy and mass "are interchangeable; they are different forms of the same thing" (Nova, n.d.). Under the right conditions, mass can become energy, and vice versa. Not only that, a small amount of mass can be converted into a tremendous amount of energy. The speed of light, after all, is a very large number (299,792,458 meters per second): and it is mc squared. That is mass multiplied by 89,875,517,873,681,764 meters per second.

When Einstein developed his equation, the possibility of nuclear fission was still unrealized, and the conversion of matter to energy remained theoretical. However, Einstein's theories held that if scientists could find a way to convert matter into energy, the amount of energy that would be produced would be extraordinary indeed.

Energy can be utilized for different purposes. On one hand, energy can be used to power machines, to light homes, and to heat buildings. On the other hand, if a huge amount of energy is unleashed simultaneously, it would produce a gigantic explosion, sufficient to level cities and kill tens of thousands of people. Einstein's equation raised the possibility of a new future for the world, a new means of meeting its energy needs. But it also raised the possibility of weapons so powerful that they could demolish cities and kill thousands of people in a single stroke.

Enter Niels Bohr

Around the same time that H. G. Wells was

writing his 1914 novel, *The World Set Free,* Niels Bohr was publishing his immensely influential model of atomic structure.

Niels Bohr was a Danish physicist with a Jewish ancestry, born in Copenhagen, Denmark on October 7, 1885. His mother came from a rich Jewish banking family, and his father was a professor of physiology at the University of Copenhagen. On August 1, 1912, he married the love of his life, Margrethe Nørlund, with whom he had six children.

An insight into Bohr's character and his infamous absentmindedness can be taken from Lieutenant Colonel John Lansdale's report in February 1944. At this time, Bohr and his son Aage were in Los Alamos, New Mexico, where Bohr was acting as a consultant for the Manhattan Project. Lansdale writes (quoted by Wellerstein, 2015):

They did a great deal of walking, this Agent had occasion to spend considerable time behind them and observe that it was rare when either of them paid much attention to stop lights or signs, but proceeded on their way much the same as if they were walking in the wood. On one occasion, subjects proceeded across a busy intersection against the red light in a diagonal fashion, taking the longest route possible and one of greatest danger. The resourceful work of Agent Maiers in blocking out one half of the stream of automobile traffic with his car prevented their possible incurring serious injury in this instance. (para 4)

By that point, Niels Bohr was already a "living legend" (Rozsa, 2023). He won the Nobel Prize in Physics in 1922, after publishing his model of atomic structure in 1913. As science journalist Mary Bellis (2019) puts it, the Bohr model of atomic structure "became the basis for all future quantum theories."

If you remember your chemistry from school, you may be vaguely familiar with Bohr's model. Bohr's theory held that the electrons of an atom traveled in orbits around its nucleus and that the chemical properties of an element were largely determined by the number of electrons in the higher-energy, outer orbits. Bohr's model is still commonly taught in schools, despite being technically obsolete, it is relatively simple and eases students into more accurate but much more complex quantum models.

In publishing his model, Bohr was building on the work of German physicists Max Planck and Albert Einstein, and advancing the new science of quantum mechanics. The birth of quantum mechanics—which "maintains that energy is both matter and a wave, depending on certain variables" (History.com Editors, 2023)—paved the way for research into subatomic processes. In the years that followed 1913, Bohr continued to develop his model of the atom and became a champion for quantum physics.

Bohr's work in quantum theory was in academic opposition to the work of Albert Einstein. According to Einstein's famous words, "God does not play dice." Einstein criticized quantum theory, which provided a view of the world that was inherently probabilistic. Bohr, meanwhile, argued that "the mere act of indirectly observing the atomic realm changes the outcome of quantum interactions" (American Museum of Natural History, n.d.). Because of this, quantum predictions had to be made based on predictions rather than observation, resulting in a probabilistic rather than determinative model.

There is no reason to think that there was any personal animosity between Bohr and Einstein. Professor Andrew Boyd at the University of Houston notes that "Bohr and Einstein were friends and had great respect for one another" (n.d.). Nonetheless, they disagreed strongly on this point of science, and their academic rivalry came to a head at the 1927 Solvay Conference. There, Einstein and Bohr engaged in friendly but rigorous debate about quantum theory, and "by most accounts of this public debate, Bohr was the victor" (American Museum of Natural History, n.d.). It turned out that God did play with dice, after all.

In championing quantum theory, Bohr contributed to new ways of looking at the atom and modeling subatomic behaviors. And, more importantly, this research pointed in the direction of nuclear fission: the splitting of an atom into two, smaller atoms when it is bombarded by neutrons.

Realizing Nuclear Fission

For many years following Bohr's model, nuclear fission was a hypothetical but unrealized possibility. It was eventually achieved in 1938, by the German radiochemists Otto Hahn and Fritz Strassman.

Hahn and Strassman appear to have held somewhat different views about Adolf Hitler and Nazism. It must be said that Hahn worked with many Jewish scientists, both before and after the rise of Nazism, and that he opposed the persecution of Jewish people and the dismissal of his Jewish colleagues. On the other hand, in an interview Hahn gave to the Toronto Star Weekly in 1933, he does seem to praise Hitler in rather colorful terms (quoted in Sime, 2006):

I am not a Nazi. But Hitler is the hope, the powerful hope, of German youth... At least 20 million people revere him. He began as a nobody, and you see what he has become in ten years... In any case for the youth, for the nation of the future, Hitler is a hero, a Führer, a saint... In his daily life he is almost a saint. No alcohol, not even tobacco, no meat, no women. In a word: Hitler is an unequivocal Christ. (p. 6)

Hahn worked on the German nuclear weapons program throughout the war. On April 25, 1945, Hahn was arrested by members of the British and American Alsos Mission and was incarcerated with other German scientists at Farm Hall for six months. At Farm Hall, Hahn would claim that he was glad not to have succeeded in the atomic project.

By contrast, Fritz Strassman was blacklisted by the Nazi regime. When the Society of German Chemists became part of a Nazi-controlled corporation, Strassman resigned from the society and was later quoted as saying, "If my work would lead to Hitler having an atomic bomb I would kill myself" (Spartacus Educational, n.d.). Perhaps most impressive of all, Strassman and his wife Maria concealed Jewish musician Andrea Wolfenstein during the Second World War, putting themselves and their three-year-old son, Martin, at extraordinary risk of retribution from the Nazi regime.

Prevented from working as a scientist due to his political opposition to the Nazis, Strassman was eventually employed by Hahn as a special assistant on half pay to sidestep such restrictions. They worked together at Niel Bohr's institute in Copenhagen, studying what happens when uranium atoms are bombarded by neutrons. They found that they had unexpectedly created barium, a much lighter element than uranium. With the help of the Austrian-Jewish scientist Lise Meitner, they worked out what had happened using physics calculations—based on Bohr's model—and realized that nuclear fission of uranium had taken place.

For her part, Lise Meitner was only permitted to work as a scientist in 1938 because she was an Austrian, rather than a German, citizen. Nonetheless, she was soon forced to flee the persecution of the Nazis in the same year, when Germany unified with Austria through the *Anschluss* and she lost her Austrian citizenship.

With the help of Niels Bohr, she fled to Sweden, where she eventually became a citizen.

The discovery of nuclear fission raised a terrifying possibility. If the fission process became self-sustaining—with neutrons produced by fission striking other nuclei and leading to more fission—then this would form a chain reaction and produce a vast amount of energy.

In other words, it would produce an atomic explosion. The realization of nuclear fission proved that an atomic bomb was possible. And this discovery had been made in Nazi Germany.

Enter Enrico Fermi

After the discovery of nuclear fission, it was only a matter of time before scientists discovered a way to produce a self-sustaining nuclear chain reaction. The honor of creating the first neutronic reactor went to the Italian physicist, Enrico Fermi.

Fermi was born in Rome on September 29, 1901, to his father Alberto Fermi—a division head in the Ministry of Railways—and his mother Ida de Gattis, an elementary school teacher. Despite becoming a man in the shadow of the First World War and the rise of fascism, the journalist Gregg Herken (2016) notes that

"Fermi exuded an almost ethereal calm, and he remained unflappable in the face of both triumph and disaster." His colleagues nicknamed him "the Pope" due to his phenomenal scientific intuition, with one of his graduate students claiming that "Fermi had an inside track to God" (quoted in Herken, 2016). Moreover, Fermi differed from many of his peers in being equally skilled at both experimental work and theoretical physics. Indeed, he would joke about it, stating, "I could never learn to stay in bed late enough in the morning to be a theoretical physicist" (quoted in Herken, 2016).

By 1922, Fermi had earned his PhD in physics from the University of Pisa, and in 1934 he discovered the phenomenon of slow neutrons. This, in the words of the Nobel Prize website (2023), led "to the discovery of nuclear fission and the production of elements lying beyond what was until then the Periodic Table."

A slow neutron is a neutron with a kinetic energy below around 1 electron volt (eV). The relevance of slow neutrons to nuclear fission is that a slow neutron can be captured by a uranium-235 nucleus, causing the uranium to become unstable and facilitating nuclear fission. By contrast, a fast neutron will not be captured by a uranium-235 nucleus. As such, the process of slowing down a neutron is necessary for the work of fission reactors.

Unlike many of the scientists who would later work on the Manhattan Project, Fermi was not himself Jewish, but his wife, Laura Capon, was. Fermi married his wife on July 19, 1928, and left Italy ten years later, primarily because of the anti-semitic racial laws introduced by the fascist Benito Mussolini. Fermi and his family traveled to the United States, where Fermi would later become a citizen in 1944. He worked at the Chicago Metallurgical Laboratory (also known as the Chicago "Met Lab") and with his team created Chicago Pile-1, the first artificial nuclear reactor.

Chicago Pile-1, or "CP-1," was "a monolith made of carefully stacked graphite blocks, interlaced with cubes of uranium" (Grundhauser, 2016), built on a squash court beneath the Stagg Football Field at the University of Chicago. Though its successful test on December 2, 1942, heralded the Atomic Age, Cindy Kelly, president of the Atomic Heritage Foundation, notes that Fermi was characteristically relaxed: "In Fermi's words, the event was not spectacular. No fuses burned, no lights flashed" (quoted in Grundhauser,

2016). Nonetheless, the scientists did celebrate by splitting a bottle of Chianti, each signing the bottle to mark the event. The bottle can still be seen in a museum in Argonne, Illinois.

Meanwhile, the physicist Arthur Compton, who had helped build CP-1, reported the success to James Conant, chairman of the National Defense Research Committee, speaking in an improvised bit of spy code (quoted in Grundhauser, 2016):

> **Compton:** Jim, you'll be interested to know, the Italian navigator has just landed in the new world. The earth is not as large as he had estimated. He arrived at the new world sooner than he expected.
>
> **Conant:** Is that so? Were the natives friendly?
>
> **Compton:** Everyone landed safe and happy.

Not only was nuclear fission possible, but a chain reaction had also been achieved. The stage was set for the creation of the first atomic bomb.

CHAPTER 2
WORLD AT WAR

Antisemitism and the Nazi Atomic Project

November 9, 1938. *Kristallnacht:* The Night of Broken Glass.

Kristallnacht represented a violent escalation of the virulent antisemitism taking hold in Nazi Germany. Around 7,500 Jewish shops were attacked and 400 synagogues were burned to the ground. Almost 100 Jewish people were murdered, and 30,000 were sent to concentration camps (United States Holocaust Memorial Museum, 2019).

Though *Kristallnacht* lives in infamy as a particularly brutal event, the Nazis had been persecuting the Jewish community from the beginning of Hitler's rise to power. In 1933, schools began teaching German children that Jewish people were *untermensch*, or "undesirable persons." On April 1, 1933, a boycott of Jewish businesses took place, with many shops being vandalized. In 1935, the Nuremberg Laws were passed, stripping Jewish people of their German citizenship and banning marriages and relationships between Jewish people and Germans. By 1938, Jewish people had to carry identity cards identifying them as Jewish, Jewish children were banned from schools, and Jewish people had to add "Israel" or "Sarah" to their name to make it obvious that they had Jewish ancestry. *Kristallnacht* was an escalation to outright violence, but the Jewish community had been suffering for years. By 1939, the first ghettos designed to segregate Jewish people from other citizens were opened, and on November 23, 1939, Jewish people were forced to wear the Star of David on their clothes, identifying them all the more easily for persecution.

Many—almost all—of the scientists who worked on the Manhattan Project were either Jewish or had spouses who were. Adolf Hitler's rampant antisemitism was not only an appalling human rights violation, but it also shot him in the foot. His hatred of Jewish people and quantum theory (labeled a "Jewish science") would greatly hinder the German bomb project in the years to come.

In 1939, Poland was invaded by Nazi Germany, and the United Kingdom and France declared war. The Second World War had begun and would claim 70 to 85 million lives, mostly civilians. The Nazis would perpetrate the Holocaust, attempting genocide against the Jewish peoples of the world.

Against this backdrop of world war, it must be remembered that nuclear fission was realized by German scientists: Otto Hahn and Fritz Strassman. One of the main pioneers of quantum theory was Werner Heisenberg, another German scientist, and later the principal scientist on the German bomb project, or *Uranverein*. There was a very real fear that the Nazis would be the first to develop the atomic bomb, and this acted as a catalyst for the Manhattan Project in the United States.

Born on December 5, 1901, Werner Heisenberg was a German theoretical physicist. He worked with Niels Bohr at the University of Copenhagen from 1924 to 1925, and, in 1932, he won the Nobel Prize in Physics "for the creation of quantum mechanics" (The Nobel Prize, n.d.).

Though Heisenberg was not himself Jewish, he faced persecution for his affiliations with quantum mechanics and the theory of relativity—which of course was associated with the Jewish scientist, Albert Einstein. After Hitler came to power in 1933, Heisenberg was attacked by the German press as a "white Jew," that is, an Aryan who acted like a Jew. He faced particular hostility from the *Deutsche Physik*, or "German Physics" movement, which was supremely opposed to theoretical physics. The *Deutsche Physik* movement successfully blocked Heisenberg from becoming a professor for several years. Moreover, threats to make Heisenberg "disappear" were made in *Das Schwarze Korps*, the newspaper of the SS—the Nazi Security Service, or *Sicherheitsdienst*—and Heinrich Himmler: The man now known as the principal architect of the Holocaust.

If not for a quirk of fate, Heisenberg may have been another victim of the Nazi regime, or else forced to flee Nazi Germany. However, Heisenberg's mother, Annie Wecklein, happened to know Himmler's mother, Anna Himmler. The two women knew each other through a Bavarian hiking club, where Heisenberg's maternal grandmother and Himmler's father were rectors and members. Based on this association, Annie Wecklein visited Anna Himmler, and soon after the matter was settled. On July 21, 1938, Heinrich Himmler sent a letter to SS Gruppenführer Reinhard Heydrich and Heisenberg, making clear that Heisenberg was of use to German science, but warning Heisenberg to be careful about his associations (quoted in Manjunath, 2021):

Because you were recommended by my family I have had your case investigated with special care and precision. I am glad that I can now inform you that I do not approve of the attack... and that I have taken measures against any further attack against you. (para 4)

P.S. I consider it, however, best if in the future you make a distinction for your audience between the results of scientific research and the personal and political attitude of the scientists involved. (para 10)

With the protection of Himmler, Heisenberg became one of the principal scientists in the German atomic bomb program, the *Uranverein.*

It is unclear to what extent Heisenberg supported the Nazi regime. When he was incarcerated at Farm Hall in 1945, his conversations with other German scientists were secretly recorded. These recordings suggest that Heisenberg was glad that the Allies had won the Second World War. In addition, there is some evidence to support the idea that Heisenberg had focused on atomic energy during his time in the *Uranverein*, rather than working on an atomic bomb (Beyler, n.d.). He told his fellow scientists at Farm Hall as much, and, when he learned about the attack on Hiroshima, he admitted that he had never calculated what the critical mass of an atomic bomb would be. As an exercise, he attempted those calculations at Farm Hall and made major errors, suggesting that he was indeed making those calculations for the first time—further supporting the idea that he was never truly working on an atomic weapon from the beginning. Furthermore, Heisenberg never joined the Nazi Party and faced constant persecution from the Nazis for years.

On the other hand, Heisenberg was part of the *Uranverein*, and we cannot be certain of his true motivations. American historian Paul Rose blames "bad physics and bad morals" (reported by Eckert, 2001) for Heisenberg's flawed contribution to the German atomic bomb project. Though Heisenberg and other German scientists would go on to explain their failures as deliberate sabotage, we must recognize that this is a convenient explanation that both protected their reputation as scientists and distanced themselves from the atrocities of the Nazi regime.

We will probably never really know to what extent Heisenberg was complicit. However, we do know that his involvement in the *Uranverein* was alarming to many scientists in the global community (Harrington, 2023). The fear of the Nazi atomic bomb was very real and would lead no less of a figure than Albert Einstein to write directly to the President of the United States, Franklin D. Roosevelt.

A Letter to the President

Hungarian physicist Leo Szilárd had theories about the atomic bomb as early as September 12, 1933, five years before nuclear fission had been realized by Hahn and Strassman. Szilárd had read H. G. Wells's novel, The World Set Free, and conceived "of a nuclear chain reaction as a way to simultaneously release and harness the energy contained in atoms" (Palese, 2019).

Leo Szilárd would later work on the Manhattan Project in Chicago, and be a constant thorn in the side of those who wished to use the bomb. He argued that the atomic bomb should be used in a peaceful demonstration to intimidate Japan into surrender, rather than being employed against civilian targets, and drafted petitions among Manhattan Project scientists urging against the use of atomic weapons and the dangers of nuclear proliferation (such as Szilárd 1945).

We'll return to Leo Szilárd in much more detail in Chapter 6, and his political efforts in the 1940s against the violent use of the atomic bomb. However, in the 1930s, Leo Szilárd was one of the main voices in favor of an American atomic bomb project.

Leo Szilárd was a Jewish man who lived in Germany from 1919, enrolling at the University of Berlin in 1921 and earning his PhD in August 1922. He completed his postdoctoral work at the Kaiser Wilhelm Institute in Berlin. When Hitler came to power in 1933, Szilárd fled antisemitic persecution and relocated to the United Kingdom, eventually moving to New York and becoming an American citizen in 1940.

It is this background that helps explain Szilárd's support for an American atomic bomb project in 1939. Szilárd feared that the Nazis would build the bomb first, and had seen firsthand the atrocities of the Nazi regime. In Szilárd's mind, there was no choice: The Americans had to build the bomb first, or else the Nazis would unleash ever greater atrocities on the world.

Fearing the Nazi atomic bomb, Szilárd approached Albert Einstein. Szilárd had become close friends with Einstein at the Kaiser Wilhelm Institute, and Einstein had become a world-renowned scientist after publishing his theory of relativity. However, the reason Szilárd approached Einstein was less about his credentials and more about his connections: Albert Einstein personally knew the Queen of Belgium, Elisabeth of Bavaria.

The reason this mattered was because of uranium. Szilárd knew that any atomic bomb would need uranium, but the element is rare. One of the biggest sources of uranium in the world is in the Congo, which—in 1939—was under the rule of Belgian imperialism. Szilárd hoped that Einstein would convince the Queen of Belgium to prevent any exports of uranium to Nazi Germany, thus halting the Nazi atomic project in its tracks.

When it came to it, Einstein was unwilling to write directly to the Queen of Belgium, feeling it improper, but he did write to the Belgian ambassador. Moreover, Einstein agreed to sign a letter drafted to President Franklin D. Roosevelt of the United States, warning the

Americans of the danger that atomic weapons posed to the Allies. At this stage, Nazi Germany was no longer exporting uranium from its Czechoslovakian mines, a surefire indication to Einstein and Szilárd that they were working on an atomic bomb.

The letter is to the point and straightforward. It warns Roosevelt that large amounts of uranium could "lead to the construction of bombs, and it is conceivable—though much less certain—that extremely powerful bombs of this type may thus be constructed" (Einstein, 1939). However, even Einstein (1939) did not foresee the full possibilities of atomic weaponry: "A single bomb of this type, carried by boat and exploded in a port, might very well destroy the whole port together with some of the surrounding territory. However, such bombs might very well prove too heavy for transportation by air."

In addition to a warning, the letter to Roosevelt included a call to action. The United States did not have much in the way of sources for uranium, and so the letter urged the American government to begin securing uranium ore as a matter of priority. It also asked Roosevelt to provide funding to universities working on atomic energy and to appoint someone who could manage an atomic weapons project.

The letter was sent on August 15, 1939, to be hand-delivered by a close friend of Roosevelt, the economist Alexander Sachs. Historian Richard Rhodes (1986) quotes Sachs as believing that he was "the right person to make the relevant scientific material intelligent to Mr. Roosevelt. No scientist could sell it to him."

In addition, there was a real concern that any letter sent by mail could be caught up in the Washington bureaucracy. According to Sachs (Rhodes, 1986):

Our social system is such that any public figure [is] punch-drunk with printer's ink... This was a matter that the Commander in Chief and the head of the Nation must know. I could only do it if I could see him for a long stretch and read the material so it came in by way of the ear and not as a soft mascara on the eye. (p. 309)

Unfortunately, however, the outbreak of the Second World War made it difficult for Sachs to secure a meeting with Roosevelt. The letter was not delivered until October 11, 1939, when Sachs finally met with the President. Sachs told Roosevelt, "Personally I think there is no doubt that subatomic energy is available all around us, and that one day man will release and control its almost infinite power. We cannot prevent him from doing so and can only hope that he will not use it exclusively in blowing up his next door neighbor" (Rhodes, 1986). According to Sachs, Roosevelt's reply was extremely to the point (Atomic Heritage Foundation, 2017): "Alex, what you are after is to see the Nazis don't blow us up."

Einstein and Szilárd's letter to the President seems to have been vital in accelerating the creation of the Manhattan Project. A letter was sent back on October 17, 1939, by Roosevelt's secretary, Edwin M. Watson, stating that the President had appointed a committee to look into the matter (U.S. Department of Energy, n.d.). By the end of summer 1942, Colonel Leslie Groves of the Army Corps of Engineers headed up the new project. At first, this project was to be called the Development of Substitute Materials, but its headquarters were in Manhattan, and it soon became known as the Manhattan District. From there, it started to take on a new name: The Manhattan Project.

An Overstated Fear

Einstein later had cause to regret his letter to Roosevelt, stating "Had I known that the Germans would not succeed in developing an atomic bomb, I would have done nothing for the bomb" (Atomic Heritage Foundation, 2017). As it was, Einstein was refused the security clearance to work on the Manhattan Project, due to his left-leaning, pacifist views. The starting gun had been fired, and Einstein no longer had any influence over where the race would go.

The truth is that Nazi Germany was greatly hamstrung by its antisemitic views regarding theoretical physics—including many of the theoretical physicists who championed quantum theory. As such, the Nazis "never came remotely close to developing" an atomic bomb (Atomic Heritage Foundation, 2017).

The *Uranverein* project had relatively little governmental support from the Nazi regime and was budgeted a mere eight million Reichsmarks, equivalent to around two million U.S. dollars at the time (Academic Accelerator, n.d.). By comparison, the American government spent 2.2 billion dollars on the Manhattan Project: over a thousand times more money. At its peak, the Manhattan Project consisted of 130,000 workers. The *Uranverein* had less than 100 people working on the project. Werner Heisenberg would later remark (quoted by Macrakis, 1993) that "we wouldn't have had the moral courage to recommend to the government in the spring of 1942 that they should employ 120,000 men just for building the thing up."

When it came to it, then, the Nazi atomic bomb project was a fraction of the size of the Manhattan Project, and fears of a Nazi atomic bomb were greatly overstated. However, it is easy to know this in hindsight. Despite the limitations of the *Uranverein* project, it was fear of a Nazi atomic bomb—of Adolf Hitler having access to the most powerful weapon in history— that galvanized the Manhattan Project and led to the creation of the first atomic weapon.

The race for the atomic bomb had begun.

CHAPTER 3
THE MANHATTAN PROJECT'S GENESIS

The General

After Einstein and Szilárd warned the United States about the possibility of a Nazi atomic bomb, the American atomic project went into overdrive. The Manhattan Engineer District (MED) was formally established on August 16, 1942. It was deemed that the MED needed aggressive leadership to drive productivity, and then-Colonel Leslie Groves of the Army Corps of Engineers was selected. He was swiftly promoted to brigadier general—it was felt that the scientists of the Manhattan Project would respect a general more than a colonel—and would later become a major general on March 9, 1944.

Groves was born on August 17, 1896, to a United States Army chaplain, Leslie Richard Groves Sr., and his wife Gwen Groves née Griffith. He moved constantly during his childhood as a result of his father's military career: from Vancouver to Minnesota, to New Jersey, back to Minnesota, and then to Altadena. Furthermore, there was never a doubt in Groves's mind that he would follow in his father's militaristic footprints. After previously failing the entrance test, Groves was admitted to the United States Military Academy (USMA), also known as West Point, in 1916. Finishing fourth in his class, Groves earned a commission as a second lieutenant in the Corps of Engineers and was promoted to first lieutenant on May 1, 1919. By November 14, 1940, he had been made a colonel.

By the time of the Manhattan Project, Groves already had a reputation for being a doer. He had just overseen the project to build the Pentagon between 1941 and 1942. A project that was beset with crises, Groves was tasked with fixing them, and joked that he was "hoping to get to a war theater so I could find a little peace" (quoted in Fine & Remington, 1972).

Despite the prestige and importance of the

Manhattan Project, Groves was disappointed not to be sent to a war theater. He was a bullish and direct man and saw his role as someone who would cut through the chaff and make decisions. In an interview with Stephane Groueff in 1965, Groves lamented the hand-wringing and slow decision-making that had become commonplace in the 60s (Atomic Heritage Foundation, Groves & Groueff, 1965a):

That is the big difference between the way that we operated and the way that things are generally done today. If you think of all the time that is spent in the preparation of reports and studies and economic analyses and money costs and all the rest of it today in the slightest decision, that is why they cannot get anything done. Now, actually, you save money as well as time, and you get a better product if you do not hesitate so much. (para 125)

Groves's approach would sometimes irritate scientists on the Manhattan Project, who favored a more contemplative approach. But, for Groves, the project had to progress swiftly if the United States were to beat the Nazis to a bomb, and he was happy "to make the decisions when they had to be made... irrespective of how much data was available" (Groves, 1965a).

As it was, Groves was unafraid of being

disliked or criticized. When warned that Oppenheimer would say unpleasant things behind his back, Groves brushed it off as the normal griping made by subordinates toward their superior officers. Similarly, if he needed to talk to someone about a matter of importance, he would call them directly rather than going through their superiors, no matter how much this irritated their superiors (Groves, 1965d):

> I would never call a man who had to ask somebody else if I could help it. I wanted to talk to the man who knew. Then my philosophy was that it was that man's responsibility to inform his superiors of our phone call and what he had said if they want him to. It caused a lot of trouble because people didn't like it. (para 162)

Groves's bullish attitude was not just toward scientists and fellow military personnel, however. He also had no qualms about talking to United States senators, stating that he was more than willing "to give an impression to them that you know exactly what you are talking about and that you are as big a man or bigger than they are" (Groves, 1965a). In many ways, Groves was the perfect man for the job. He could drive the Manhattan Project at an aggressive pace, cut through delays and committees, and defend the funding allocated to the project from senators and other politicians. He was also scientifically competent, having trained as an army engineer for over ten years.

Nonetheless, he would need scientists of absolute brilliance to achieve the making of the atomic bomb.

The Father of the Atomic Bomb

Many esteemed scientists worked on the Manhattan Project. Some had Nobel Prizes. But it was Oppenheimer who was made director of the project and became the "Father of the Atomic Bomb", a man without a Nobel Prize and with a problematic history of supporting left-wing causes (Speicher, 2023).

Despite his lack of a Nobel Prize—Groves's view that it was simply harder to get a Nobel Prize as a theoretical rather than experimental physicist—Oppenheimer undoubtedly possessed a brilliant mind. He learned Sanskrit at the age of 30, simply as a hobby. When on a visit to the Netherlands, he learned enough Dutch in six weeks to be able to deliver a technical lecture in the language. As the New York Times (1967) would write in his obituary, the man had an "almost compulsive avidity for learning."

Oppenheimer was born in New York City on

April 22, 1904, into a non-observant Jewish family. He was also born into considerable wealth. Though his father Julius had emigrated to the United States with nothing, he had become an executive of a successful textile company.

By the time of the Manhattan Project, Oppenheimer was a respected scientist and professor at the University of California in Berkeley. He made significant contributions to theoretical physics, contributing to championing the development of quantum mechanics and nuclear physics, as well as working on theories of black holes and neutron stars, the interactions of cosmic rays, and quantum field theory.

He was also something of a polarizing figure. The New York Times (1967) writes:

He was Oppy, Oppie or Opje to hundreds of persons who were captivated by his charm, eloquence and sharp, subtle humor and who were awed by the scope of his erudition, the incisiveness of his mind, the chill of his sarcasm and his arrogance toward those he thought were slow or shoddy thinkers... He was extremely fidgety when he sat, and he constantly shifted himself in his chair, bit his knuckles, scratched his head and crossed and uncrossed his legs.

When he spoke on his feet, he paced and stalked, smoking incessantly and jerking a cigarette or pipe out of his mouth almost violently when he wanted to emphasize a word or phrase with a gesture. (para 24 & 26)

Throughout his career, Oppenheimer would make some powerful enemies, and this would later prove to be his downfall. Though he got along well enough with Groves, he would endlessly irritate the general by not taking security procedures seriously enough. But he also had his admirers. Many of his students were utterly devoted to him, copying his mannerisms and even relocating across the country to follow the professor.

Most controversial of all, however, were his political associations. By his own admission, he was not interested in politics until late 1936, by which time he had become involved in various communist, trade union, and liberal causes. In his own words (quoted in the New York Times, 1967),

I had had a continuing smoldering fury about the treatment of Jews in Germany. I had relatives there, and was later to help in extricating them and bringing them to this country. I saw what the Depression was doing to my students. Often they could get no jobs, or jobs which were wholly inadequate. And through them, I began to understand how deeply political and economic events could affect men's lives. I began to feel the need to participate more fully in the life of the community. (para 54)

These causes included Oppenheimer sending $500 through communist channels to help fund socialist ambulances in the Spanish Civil War (Nichols, 1954).

Oppenheimer's left-wing associations also followed him into his personal life. He had a passionate affair with communist and psychiatrist in training, Jean Tatlock, from 1936 to 1941, proposing to her twice and being rejected on both occasions. His wife, Kitty Harrison—whom he married in November 1940—had previously been a member of the Communist Party of America, and was the widow of Joseph Dallet, an American communist who died fighting in the Spanish Civil War.

Groves, however, was fairly relaxed about Oppenheimer's background, stating the following in an interview with Groueff (1965b):

During the Depression years, and during the Spanish War, all the liberals in this country and almost everybody, excepting what might be termed a hard-core five or ten percent, were in favor of the Spanish Communists winning. They saw nothing wrong with communism, they approved of the recognition of Russia by Roosevelt. They had no fears of communism. They thought it was just as nice as anything else could be. (para 119)

Groves also downplayed the donation of $500 to the communist side of the Spanish Civil War. Though it was a fair amount of money—over $9000 in today's money—Oppenheimer was so rich that such an amount of money would have meant very little to him. As Groves put it, based on his investments, Oppenheimer probably had a salary larger than the president of Berkeley.

Moreover, it seems that Groves simply liked Oppenheimer. He later stated that Oppenheimer was "very pleasant, if you do not have any resentment toward the man who was totally different from what you are, in every way" (Groves, 1965b). Groves wanted Oppenheimer to direct the project because Oppenheimer had a breadth of scientific knowledge that was unusual among the hyper-specialized scientists of the Manhattan Project, and also because Groves detected in

Oppenheimer an "overweening ambition" (Norris, 2002) that would push the project forward. With these considerations in mind, Groves fast-tracked Oppenheimer's security clearance. In a statement that is entirely characteristic of the man, Groves felt confident in his decision, noting that "It was not difficult. No decision is difficult" (Groves, 1965b).

With Oppenheimer, the Manhattan Project had its director. But this was only one part of the puzzle. Many scientists would have to be recruited to America's atomic bomb program, and entirely new towns would have to be constructed for the work to be conducted.

Practical Concerns

At its peak, the Manhattan Project had a staff of around 130,000 people. Though many of these individuals were construction workers, service providers, and military personnel, there was a tremendous push to employ hundreds of scientists who could advance the atomic bomb project—and could also be granted a security clearance.

One of the major obstacles to recruiting scientists was the need for absolute security. Oppenheimer had to recruit scientists for the project without being able to tell them where they would be working, how long they would be working on the project, or even the full details of what they would be working on. In an interview with Stephane Groueff (Atomic Heritage Foundation, 1965), Oppenheimer notes that "it was not trivial to persuade people that this was real." Oppenheimer traveled with Groves all over the country—in particular the Metallurgical Laboratory in Chicago and the Radiation Laboratory in Berkeley—to convince scientists to join the project.

In addition to the problem of recruitment, there were huge demands on infrastructure. Due to the secrecy of the project, three entirely new cities had to be built for the Manhattan Project, to house the personnel who would be working on the bomb, and to make room for laboratories and factories necessary for the project. These cities did not appear on any map, were known as "X," "Y," and "Z" on reports, and were eventually home to around 125,000 people, including families and young children.

These cities were Hanford, Oak Ridge, and Los Alamos.

Hanford is situated in the desert of Washington State. It was established on January 16, 1943, and chosen as the site where plutonium would be created for the atomic project. Oak Ridge, situated in the hills of eastern Tennessee, would contain the Y-12 and K-25 plants for producing enriched uranium. And Los Alamos in northern New Mexico—the site of the Trinity test—would act as a site for experimental and theoretical research under the direction of Oppenheimer.

In the case of Los Alamos, an entire town (later a city) had to be built from scratch. The only building in Los Alamos was a boarding school for rich east-coast kids. Houses, laboratories, schools, and shops had to be constructed, as well as military buildings and a military perimeter to guard the site. This is not to dismiss the infrastructural challenges posed by Hanford and Oak Ridge, however. Entire uranium plants had to be built in a matter of months: an immense, engineering challenge to be tackled by the Army Corps of Engineers.

As the main site of research into the atomic bomb and the place where the Trinity test would take place, Los Alamos is the most famous of the sites created for the Manhattan Project. However, it was not the only place of research, with the Chicago Met Lab also contributing major research under the auspices of Enrico Fermi and Leo Szilárd. On the other hand, where Fermi and Szilárd were conducting their research under the Chicago University football field, the scientists and researchers of Los Alamos and Oak Ridge were living in places that, at first, resembled frontier towns. Philip S. Anderson Jr., the son of an officer in the U.S. Army Corps of Engineers, lived at Oak Ridge from second grade to junior year of high school (Anderson, 2018). He describes a frontier town with mud and boardwalks, sidewalks only following much later.

Liane B. Russell is a renowned geneticist who worked on determining radiation-induced mutation rates in mice at Oak Ridge and helped discover that the Y chromosome determines biological sex. She moved to Oak Ridge with her husband William L. Russell in 1947 and offers an even more negative view of the accommodations. She describes the buildings at Oak Ridge that served as houses (Russell, 2018):

They were miserable-looking things. They were like plywood boxes. They had no windows; they had shutters that you had to open to get air. They had no plumbing; there were separate bathhouses. They had one central little pot-bellied stove. Really bad. (para 46)

In addition to the problem of actually building the sites at Hanford, Oak Ridge, and Los Alamos, there was a great deal of work done first in choosing the sites. In discussing the selection of Los Alamos, Groves (Groves, 1965c) notes that the sites had to be places that could be kept secret, had room for considerable expansion, and yet were not too isolated to create logistical problems.

For example, before Los Alamos was suggested, the original site was supposed to be an area near Albuquerque. But it had several problems. When Groves visited the site with Oppenheimer and Major John Dudley, he saw at once that there was no room for expansion. Furthermore, it had a considerable population of Native Americans already living in the area, a population that would have to be expelled if the area was to be used for the Manhattan Project. Groves considered that this would make it difficult to conceal the existence of the site, on the basis that such an expulsion would be bound to attract a lot of attention.

In the end, Los Alamos was suggested by Oppenheimer, who owned a nearby ranch with his brother Frank. Rather than waste the day examining the doomed site near Albuquerque, the three men traveled to the Los Alamos school and found that the area was suitable. In addition to having room to expand and being relatively easy to keep secret, Los Alamos also had a preexisting road that Groves personally judged to be robust. It would have to be: A great deal of construction material would be transported along it.

In addition to these infrastructural and logistical concerns, Oppenheimer was also thinking about the morale of scientists on the Manhattan Project. When interviewed in 1965 about the choice of Los Alamos, Oppenheimer noted that "if you are going to ask people to be essentially confined, you must not put them in the bottom of a canyon. You have to put them on the top of a mesa. I think that was even more important than the technical details" (Oppenheimer, 1965).

Despite these considerations, Oppenheimer was under no illusion about what he was asking the scientists on the Manhattan Project to do. Oppenheimer was asking them to come out into the middle of the desert and stay there for an undetermined amount of time. Oppenheimer would later tell the story of physicist Emilio Segrè arriving in Los Alamos in April 1943. The two men "looked out over the desert and to the Sangre de Cristo, which were covered with snow. It was extremely beautiful. And Segrè said, 'We are going to get to hate this view'" (Oppenheimer, 1965).

In addition to these three major concerns,

there were other, esoteric factors that Groves and Oppenheimer had to consider. For example, Hanford had an economically important river running through the site, teeming with freshwater salmon. If the site at Hanford disrupted the salmon, this would cripple the local economy. Moreover, as Groves later reflected, the death of the salmon would have the impact of "scaring the country to death" (Groves, 1965c) about the research being done. With these concerns in mind, the Corps of Engineers spent around ten million dollars to construct fish elevators and fish ladders, to protect the local salmon population and the local economy.

Despite these issues, Hanford, Oak Ridge, and Los Alamos were built in an intensely short amount of time. Scientists and other personnel working on the Manhattan Project were rehomed at these sites, and the real scientific work could begin.

Compartmentalization and Spying

Compartmentalization was a critical feature of the security apparatus Groves had constructed around the Manhattan Project. It was the idea that no one working on the Manhattan Project should know any more about the project than was strictly necessary. Though this had little meaning to high-level theorists and directors like Oppenheimer, many people working on the Manhattan Project did not even know that the project was developing an atomic bomb. Even scientists—who would have likely had their suspicions about the project's goals, if they had not gossiped about it already—were not allowed to share their findings with colleagues working on other technical problems. This way, a spy or traitor was not in the position to give away all the secrets of the Manhattan Project to another country.

The issue of security was very real. When traveling to Chicago, Groves would take extraordinary measures to prevent classified documents from being stolen from his person. When on the train, he would keep his files in a brown envelope under his mattress, reasoning that a brown envelope looks less enticing than a briefcase. He would lock the compartment and wear civilian clothes to avoid drawing attention to himself. And he would carry around a pistol, loose in his trouser pocket, just in case anything happened.

At this stage in American history, military authorities were worried about espionage from both Soviet Russia and Nazi Germany. Oppenheimer, due to his left-wing associations, was constantly wiretapped and followed by the security services. As already noted, Einstein was prevented from working on the project due to his left-wing, pacifist politics. The movement of scientists at Los Alamos and other sites was carefully monitored, with identity cards and security clearances becoming a normal part of life working on the Manhattan Project.

And yet, despite all these efforts, the Soviets did manage to infiltrate the Manhattan Project.

Klaus Fuchs was a German theoretical physicist, born to a Lutheran pastor, Emil Fuchs, and his wife Else Wagner. His father had served in the army during the First World War but had since become a pacifist and a socialist, joining the Social Democratic Party of Germany (SPD) in 1921. Klaus Fuchs would inherit these political views, joining the student branch of the SPD in 1930.

Just as it was not safe to be Jewish in 1930s Germany, German communists faced persecution and ruin from Hitler's rise to power. Fuchs left Germany in 1933, after Hitler became Chancellor, and did not return until after the Second World War. He fled to Britain, and later worked in the Theoretical Physics Division at the Los Alamos site, from August 1944. By this time, he had already offered to spy for the Soviet

Union.

It is unclear to what extent Fuchs's spy activities influenced the course of history. The historian Frank Close claims in his 2019 book that "it was primarily Fuchs who enabled the Soviets to catch up with Americans" in the nuclear arms race, but the historian David Holloway notes in his 1994 book that the pace of the Soviet nuclear project was primarily set by the amount of uranium it could procure.

Either way, Fuchs confessed in early 1950, after decrypted messages revealed Fuchs's communications with the Russians. He was charged by British authorities with violating the Official Secrets Act and sentenced to fourteen years in prison. He served nine years of this sentence before his release in 1959 when he finally returned to East Germany and remained there for the rest of his life.

CHAPTER 4
ARCHITECTS OF DESTINY

An Embarrassment of Riches

To begin the Manhattan Project, the United States needed scientists of an extraordinary caliber. Groves and Oppenheimer would travel across the country—and beyond—to recruit researchers and theoretical physicists for the atomic bomb project, and gather a collection of scientists who were unmatched in their technical abilities.

As director of the project, there was of course Oppenheimer himself. As noted in the last chapter, he was a genius with a tremendous capacity for learning and a huge breadth of scientific knowledge. He could contribute to a wide range of scientific discussions on the atomic project, and so was perfect for directing the overall endeavor.

In his interview with Stephane Groueff (Groves, 1965b), Groves speaks candidly about Oppenheimer's abilities and limitations:

He had a wide experience in theoretical physics and it showed in everything he said. I quickly learned that he had no experience in administration and had no particular qualifications for administration in any way. In fact, you would have thought of him as a cloistered professor type. I was appealed to by his great grasp of everything. I was appalled by his ignorance of American history, military history, anything pertaining to operation[s] of this kind... Oppenheimer's great mental capacity impressed me, I think, when he told me that he had learned Sanskrit just for the fun of it. (para 49-50)

Moreover, despite his lack of experience, Oppenheimer turned out to be a highly skilled administrator. The New York Times obituary of Oppenheimer notes that he "displayed a special genius for administration, for handling the sensitive prima-donna scientific staff (often he spent as much time on personal as on professional problems) and for coordinating its work" (1967).

Indeed, Oppenheimer fit in well with the remarkable scientific community he gathered for the Manhattan Project. Like many of his contemporaries and colleagues, he was independently wealthy, well-traveled, and politically naive. Having traveled all over the world to attend scientific conferences and discuss high-level physics, regardless of nationality, race, or creed, Oppenheimer and his colleagues did not live in a world of nationalistic borders or ordinary political problems. They lived in a world of global cooperation that did not reflect the experience of ordinary people's lives. This may well have contributed to a certain naivety about the atomic bomb and its potential governance.

Despite their political idealism and naivety, the caliber of the scientists who worked on the Manhattan Project was undoubtedly impressive. The Manhattan Project boasted eight Nobel Prize winners at the time of the project, listed below in order of award:

- **Niels Bohr** (Physics, 1922, for his model of the atom)
- **James Franck** (Physics, 1925, for his experiments supporting Bohr's theory of atomic structure)

- **Arthur Compton** (Physics, 1927, for the discovery of the Compton effect, in which there is a decrease of energy from a photon interacting with a charged particle)
- **Harold Urey** (Chemistry, 1934, for the discovery of deuterium, a hydrogen isotope later used in the H-bomb)
- **James Chadwick** (Physics, 1935, for the discovery of neutrons, non-charged particles in atoms)
- **Enrico Fermi** (Physics, 1938, for the discovery of how to create radioactive isotopes by bombarding atoms with neutrons)
- **Ernest Lawrence** (Physics, 1939, for the invention of the cyclotron, a device that uses electromagnetic fields to speed up protons for the production of isotopes)
- **Isidor Isaac Rabi** (Physics, 1944, for inventing a technique using molecular beams to study the magnetic properties of nuclei)

Moreover, an additional twenty-three of the project's scientists would later be awarded a Nobel Prize after the Second World War, mostly for Physics.

Oppenheimer did not have a Nobel Prize himself—he was nominated three times, in 1945, 1951, and 1967, but never won. This was considered a potential problem, as it was feared that without a Nobel Prize, Oppenheimer would not have the authority to direct other scientists on the project. As it turned out, scientific clout was not the problem. Instead, most of Oppenheimer's administrative difficulties were the result of interpersonal drama between scientists in the project.

The Drama of Theoretical Physics

Though Oppenheimer was a genius, he could not develop the atomic bomb alone. At Los Alamos and the Chicago Met Lab, a great number of theoretical physicists worked on the project, and they did not always get along.

Edward Teller was a Hungarian-born theoretical physicist whose later work would lead to the creation of the hydrogen bomb (or "H-bomb") after the success of the Manhattan Project. Like Oppenheimer, he was born to wealthy, Jewish parents, but was not particularly observant of the Jewish faith. Also like Oppenheimer, he was a polarizing figure. Teller was notoriously prickly and difficult to get along with. While at Los Alamos, he insisted on working on his H-bomb instead of the project at hand, and at one point in the Manhattan Project outright "refused to engage in calculations for the implosion mechanism of the fission [atomic] bomb" (Atomic Heritage Foundation, n.d.a).

Part of the problem with Teller was that he felt passed over for the role of Director of the Theoretical Division at Los Alamos. That honor went instead to Hans Bethe, a German-American theoretical physicist and close friend of both Teller and Oppenheimer. As with most of the scientists on the Manhattan Project, Bethe was born into wealth and had Jewish ancestry on his mother's side. Unlike Teller, however, he was level-headed and patient. Jogalekar (2014) notes that this surely factored into Oppenheimer's decision to make Bethe Director of the Theoretical Division over Teller:

Oppenheimer's decision was wise; he had sized up both physicists and realized that while both were undoubtedly scientifically capable, administering a division of prima donnas needed steadfast determination, levelheaded decision making and the ability to be a team player while quietly soothing egos, all of which were qualities inherent in Bethe but not in the volatile Teller. (para 8)

We might say that Teller—in later refusing to do the work he was asked to do—proved

Oppenheimer right. Not only that, but it resulted in Klaus Fuchs—a man who was an active spy for the Soviet Union—doing his work instead.

Teller felt slighted by Bethe's promotion. He had been involved in the American atomic project from the beginning. He drove Szilárd to the meeting with Einstein which led to the letter that was sent to Roosevelt. He was an early member of the Manhattan Project while Bethe only arrived later. And he was undoubtedly worthy of the position in terms of scientific acumen. If only Teller had been less volatile and easier to manage, he might well have been made Director of the Theoretical Division.

Sadly, Teller never forgave Oppenheimer or Bethe. He had once been best friends with Bethe, but their relationship deteriorated to the point that Oppenheimer was forced to remove Teller from Bethe's Theoretical Division and place him directly under Oppenheimer's authority. Teller continued to work on the H-bomb—which he called the "Super"—causing further animosity at Los Alamos and irritating other physicists at the site. He would also contribute to Oppenheimer's political problems after the war, testifying against Oppenheimer in the hearings that led to the director's security clearance being denied.

The Chicago Metallurgical Lab

While interpersonal drama raged at Los Alamos alongside great leaps in theoretical physics, the Chicago Metallurgical Lab (or "Met Lab") was barely more functional. There, Enrico Fermi and Leo Szilárd were busy constructing Chicago Pile-1, the first artificial nuclear reactor, and contributed further research to the development of the atomic bomb. Though they worked together fruitfully, Richard Rhodes writes in the University of Chicago Magazine (2017) that their "personalities clashed."

We have already introduced Fermi and Szilárd in earlier chapters. Both had Jewish connections, either by family or by marriage, and shared a concern that Nazi Germany might develop the atomic bomb first. Enrico Fermi would later become an associate director at Los Alamos, and was present alongside Oppenheimer and Teller at the Trinity test—the first successful test of an atomic weapon.

Fermi and Szilárd's dislike of one another came from differing opinions of experimental work. Fermi was the son of a railroad inspector and was entirely content to undertake the physical work involved in "packing cans of greasy uranium oxide and mixing manganese solutions" (Rhodes, 2017). By contrast, Szilárd thought that such work was beneath his talents, and hired an assistant to do the physical labor for him. According to their mutual friend, Emilio Segrè, Fermi was offended: "Szilárd made a mortal sin... He said, 'Oh, I don't want to work and dirty my hands like a painter's assistant'" (quoted by Rhodes, 2017).

Furthermore, the two men disagreed on the role of scientists when it came to the moral implications of their work. Szilárd, a deeply conscientious man, thought that scientists had a responsibility for the social consequences of their inventions and discoveries. Fermi, meanwhile, believed that it was the role of politicians and policymakers to decide how scientific advances were utilized. In short, "Fermi thought Szilárd arrogant... Szilárd thought Fermi cynical" (Rhodes, 2017).

Szilárd's moral qualms were also upsetting the military administrators of the Manhattan Project. Though we will discuss Szilárd's ethical objections in more detail in Chapter 6, General Groves was already losing patience with Szilárd from the very beginning of the project. Szilárd "was very uneasy about the military's dominant role in managing the Manhattan Project... [and] was very vocal about these issues" (Atomic

Heritage Foundation, n.d.c). Meanwhile, his contrarian nature was causing Groves issues when it came to security and proper compartmentalization.

With this in mind, Groves found Szilárd particularly irritating among the bevy of gossiping scientists who were already giving Groves trouble. Groves would later describe Szilárd as a "thorn in the side, I think, of everyone," (Groves, 1965a)—as a troublemaker who would poison the attitude of other scientists against the military apparatus.

Certainly, Szilárd was both haughty and difficult for the Army Corps of Engineers. However, his opposition to the military use of the atomic bomb could be seen as an act of moral courage. Ultimately, like many individuals involved in the Manhattan Project, Szilárd is a controversial, polarizing figure.

The Implosion Device

Of the many technical and scientific problems that needed to be solved to complete the Manhattan Project, the most difficult were those concerning implosion.

Atomic weapons need a supercritical mass of fissile material to work—that is, material that will produce a fission chain reaction. This builds up a gigantic amount of energy, which is contained in the core of the bomb long enough to result in a nuclear explosion. However, two different kinds of atomic bombs were used on Hiroshima and Nagasaki. The bomb used on Hiroshima—known as "Little Boy"—was a gun-type fission weapon, which worked by shooting a sub-critical material into another to produce a supercritical mass. In contrast, the bomb used on Nagasaki—known as "Fat Man"—as well as the "Gadget" tested at Trinity, was an implosion-type fission weapon. As the name might suggest, this worked by compressing the fissile material into a supercritical mass through implosion. A series of detonations sent shockwaves inward, compacting the fissile material into a supercritical mass.

Compared to an implosion-type atomic weapon, the gun-type bomb "acts slower, is not as powerful, and uses far more fissile material" (Wisconsin Project on Nuclear Arms Control, n.d.). Furthermore, the gun-type bomb would not work with plutonium-239, which was comparatively easier to acquire than the uranium-235 used in the implosion-type bomb. However, the implosion-type bomb was far more difficult to design. The series of explosions that caused the implosion had to be triggered within a microsecond of each other, to ensure that the implosion was perfectly centered.

Oppenheimer, in a rare interview with Stephane Groueff (Oppenheimer, 1965), notes that implosion raised the most difficult technical problems in the Manhattan Project. Part of the issue was the difficulty of working with plutonium itself: "It gets hot, it is radioactive, you cannot touch it, you have to coat it, and the coating always peels. It is just a terrible substance" (Oppenheimer, 1965).

Research into the implosion device was one of the main focuses of the theoretical physicists involved in the Manhattan Project. Though Teller refused to work on the problem, instead focusing on his research into the H-bomb, Fermi, Bethe, and Bohr, among others worked on the initiator designs for the implosion device. A discussion listing for a May 1945 laboratory colloquium at Los Alamos outlined three initiator designs, each with a colorful name: "Urchin," attributed to James Tuck and Hans Bethe (and named for the internal spikes of the device); "Melon-Seed," attributed to James Serduke; and "Nichodemus," attributed to Niels Bohr (titled for his codename, Nicholas Baker) (Wellerstein, 2015).

Because the implosion device was so technically complex, it was the bomb design tested at Trinity. Its success, whatever its legacy, was a testament to the brilliance of the scientists who worked on the Manhattan Project, and a great scientific achievement in its own right.

CHAPTER 5
THE BRIGHT GLARE OF TRINITY

The Preliminaries

On July 16, 1945, on the plains of the Alamogordo Bombing Range—known as the Jornada del Muerto (or "Route of the Dead Man")—the world's first nuclear explosion took place.

The site was 210 miles south of Los Alamos, far from any form of civilization. It was to serve as the location for the first test of an atomic weapon, specifically, a plutonium implosion-type device of the kind that would later be dropped on Nagasaki. The test bomb, known as the "Gadget," was hoisted to the top of a 100-

foot tower, covered in wires and cables for remote detonation. We can only imagine how nervous the scientists and engineers felt as they were hoisting the Gadget upward—how much they worried about a cable snapping, and the bomb slamming into the earth. If nothing else, a gigantic amount of money was on the line.

By the time of the Trinity test, Germany and Italy had already surrendered. Italy surrendered on September 8, 1943, while Germany surrendered on May 7, 1945—just a couple of months before the test. Some scientists were already voicing concerns about the use of an atomic weapon given the state of the war. Szilárd's Franck Report had been issued from the Chicago Met Lab a month before Trinity (more on this in the next chapter). Nonetheless, the Trinity test would go ahead, and, less than a month later, the cities of Hiroshima and Nagasaki would be all but destroyed by atomic bombs.

The Trinity test was most likely named "Trinity" by Oppenheimer. Later, in 1962, Groves would write to Oppenheimer and ask why he chose the name of the test. Oppenheimer responded as follows (quoted in Rhodes, 1986):

Why I chose the name is not clear, but I know what thoughts were in my mind. There is a poem of John Donne, written just before his death, which I know and love. From it a quotation: "As West and East / In all flat Maps – and I am one – are one, / So death doth touch the Resurrection." That still does not make a Trinity, but in another, better known devotional poem Donne opens: "Batter my heart, three person'd God." (p. 571-572)

In this reply, Oppenheimer refers to the poems Hymn to God, My God, in My Sickness and Holy Sonnet XIV, both of which can be found in Poems of John Donne, Volume 1 (1896).

The site of the Trinity test was decided based on several considerations. The Alamogordo Bombing Range belonged to a United States Air Force base near Alamogordo, so the place was isolated, empty, and already in the possession of the military. It also was—and still is—a flat desert region, perfect for observation from a great distance away. Various observation shelters were built, with key observers being stationed in a control shelter around six miles away, and others observing from similar shelters either in base camp ten miles away, at Hill Station twenty miles away, or from the air in B-29 bombers (the same type of aircraft that would drop bombs on Hiroshima and

Nagasaki). Concerned about the legal liabilities of nuclear fallout, Groves also arranged for an offsite monitoring system, and put in place evacuation plans for all personnel within a forty-mile radius of the test site.

Unfortunately, these plans did not spare the residents of south New Mexico from the radioactive impact of the test. Counties downwind from the Trinity blast suffered high rates of infant mortality in the years that followed, and residents are still petitioning the United States government to take responsibility to this day (Cramer, 2020).

The original plan was for the Trinity test to take place between July 18 and 21, due to favorable weather reports, but the Potsdam Conference (between the United States, the United Kingdom, and the Soviet Union) was scheduled to begin on July 16 and then-President Harry S. Truman wanted the test to be concluded before the conference began. As such, the test was brought forward to July 16, the earliest date at which the components for the bomb would be available.

The detonation was initially planned for 04:00 MWT (Mountain Time Zone) but was delayed due to rain and lightning from earlier that morning. The fear was that rain would increase the radiation and fallout and lightning carried the risk of a premature detonation. The storm started to let up at 04:45, and the bomb was eventually detonated at 05:30.

Some Concerns

At the time of the Trinity test, the main concern among the scientists was that the bomb simply would not work. In the case of an unsuccessful explosion, a great amount of plutonium would potentially be wasted, and they would have to let Truman know that the Trinity test was a failure.

In the event of an unsuccessful explosion, there would be an effort to gather the unexploded bomb so that the plutonium could be recovered. A huge containment vessel was built under the auspices of Robert W. Henderson and Roy W. Carlson. It was a steel sphere 10 feet in diameter and 25 feet long. Its walls were 14 inches thick, and it weighed 214 short tons. Delivered partly by train, it was at the time the heaviest item ever shipped by rail. This device was called "Jumbo."

By the time of the Trinity test, the decision had already been made not to use Jumbo, as Oppenheimer was confident that there would be enough plutonium available for a second test if it came to it. Instead, it was hoisted up a steel tower 800 yards away from the atomic explosion, where it could be used for a hypothetical second test.

Jumbo survived the Trinity test, though its tower did not. Jumbo finally met its end at the hands of an Army ordnance team on April 16, 1946. It was destroyed by the detonation of eight 500 lb bombs placed at the bottom of the container.

A more colorful concern was more remote but somewhat alarming. Though Bethe had calculated that such a thing was almost impossible, Teller had previously raised the concern that a nuclear chain reaction would continue across the atmosphere. If this took place, the bomb would ignite the atmosphere and consequently incinerate the entire planet.

Perhaps to ease their anxieties about an unsuccessful explosion—or their fears about potentially destroying the world—the scientific observers set up a betting pool on the results of the Trinity test. Primarily, the betting was on the results of a successful test, with scientists betting on the explosive yield of the atomic bomb.

Teller betted the highest explosive yield, predicting the equivalent of 45 kilotons of TNT.

Norman Ramsey pessimistically betted on 0 kilotons of TNT—that is, a dud—while Oppenheimer chose 0.3 kilotons of TNT, and Bethe chose 8 kilotons of TNT. Isidor Isaac Rabi—the last scientist to arrive—chose 18 kilotons of TNT. In the end, Rabi turned out to be the winner with the closest guess.

As the scientists betted on the yield of the explosion, Fermi offered to take wagers on another possibility: whether the atmosphere would ignite, and—if it did so—whether it would destroy just New Mexico or the entire world.

The World, Forever Changed

The Trinity test did not destroy the world. But it did herald in a new era of atomic weaponry, and forever changed global politics and war.

When Oppenheimer saw the flash of light produced by the Gadget, he was reminded of the sacred Hindu text, the Bhagavad-Gita: "If the radiance of a thousand suns were to burst into the sky, that would be like the splendor of the mighty one" (quoted in the New York Times, 1967). Later, he would reflect on another passage of the Bhagavad-Gita (quoted by Sleight, 2019):

We knew the world would not be the same. A

few people laughed, a few people cried, most people were silent. I remembered the line from the Hindu scripture, the Bhagavad Gita. Vishnu is trying to persuade the prince that he should do his duty and, to impress him, takes on his multi-armed form and says, 'Now I am become Death, the destroyer of worlds.' I supposed we all felt that one way or another. (para 9)

A graduate student working on the project, Joan Hinton, described the explosion as follows (quoted in Howes & Herzenberg, 2003):

It was like being at the bottom of an ocean of light. We were bathed in it from all directions. The light withdrew into the bomb as if the bomb sucked it up. Then it turned purple and blue and went up and up and up. We were still talking in whispers when the cloud reached the level where it was struck by the rising sunlight so it cleared out the natural clouds. We saw a cloud that was dark and red at the bottom and daylight at the top. Then suddenly the sound reached us. It was very sharp and rumbled and all the mountains were rumbling with it. (line 56)

Enrico Fermi, meanwhile, described the explosion in the following way (quoted in Atomic Heritage Foundation, n.d.b):

My first impression of the explosion was the

very intense flash of light, and a sensation of heat on the parts of the body that were exposed. Although I did not directly look towards the object, I had the full impression that suddenly the countryside became brighter than in full daylight. (para 5)

Oppenheimer would later note that the success of the Trinity test, and subsequent bombings of Hiroshima and Nagasaki, had "dramatized so mercilessly the inhumanity and evil of modern war... in some sort of crude sense which no vulgarity, no humor, no overstatements can quite extinguish, the physicists have known sin; and this is a knowledge which they cannot lose" (quoted in the New York Times, 1967).

For his part, Teller was facing the nuclear explosion with sunscreen on—despite being told not to. He describes his experience in an interview uploaded to YouTube by Muon Ray (2012):

There was a very—it was early in the morning, quite dark—a very weak amount of light. I remember clearly, in the first second, my thought was 'is this all?' Then I remembered I had this heavy-ware glass on and gloves so no light could enter. So, when this light, maybe in two seconds, started to fade, I tipped my hand

and looked down at the sand. And, you know, it was as though I had removed the curtain and bright sunlight came in: then I was impressed. Then I saw the brilliant flash, not looking at it, but looking at the sand next to it.

Brigadier General Thomas F. Farrell, in his official report on the Trinity test, described the colors of the explosion's light (Farrell & Groves, n.d./1945):

The lighting effects beggared description. The whole country was lighted by a searing light with the intensity many times that of the midday sun. It was golden, purple, violet, gray, and blue. It lighted every peak, crevasse and ridge of the nearby mountain range with a clarity and beauty that cannot be described but must be seen to be imagined. (para 11)

Groves, in the same report, was similarly enthusiastic (Farrell & Groves, n.d./1945):

For the first time in history there was a nuclear explosion. And what an explosion!

There were tremendous blast effects. For a brief period there was a lighting effect within a radius of 20 miles equal to several suns in midday; a huge ball of fire was formed which lasted for several seconds. This ball mushroomed and rose to a height of over ten thousand feet before it dimmed. (para 2-3)

The explosive force of the gadget was roughly equal to 20 kilotons of TNT, or 20,000 tons. The light flash was seen over 280 miles from the test site, and the blast broke windows 120 miles away. Where the bomb had exploded, the surroundings were littered with radioactive, green glass in a radius of 330 yards, where the silica in the desert sand had melted and become what was later named trinitite. The bomb created a crater approximately 4.7 feet and 88 yards wide, and the heat wave was described as akin to an oven from as far away as base camp, with the noise of the shock wave taking 40 seconds to reach the first observers. The mushroom cloud reached 7.5 miles in height.

Military police told nearby towns that an ammunition dump had exploded.

Celebration and Awe

The reaction of the scientists and military personnel was a mix of celebration, relief, and awe. They had been working for this moment for the previous three years, expending billions of dollars, while a World War raged across the Pacific. The success of the Trinity test represented a culmination of all those efforts and expenses.

In his interview with Stephane Groueff, Groves noted that many of the scientists on the Manhattan Project had to adjust to a reality where failure had real, lasting consequences Groves, 1965d):

Before, a scientist in the academic world, if he proved something and discovered something he would become well-known scientifically and get his name in the encyclopedia and occupy a distinguished academic position. But if he failed, nobody thought anything about it. It was just as important to prove that something couldn't be done, as it was to prove that it could be done because their ambition was knowledge and knowledge is two things: first that it is possible and second that it isn't. So this was an entirely new experience because it wasn't any good for them to prove that it couldn't be done. It had to be done. And somehow, if it couldn't be done one way, they had to discover another way to accomplish it. That was the big difference. There's more feeling of responsibility that was developed than one of urgency. (para 7)

In light of this profound sense of responsibility, we can only imagine how deeply relieved the scientists were to confirm that their work had not been in vain.

Reports from the scene note that many

scientists and Manhattan Project personnel cheered and danced when the Trinity test proved to be a success. But they were also struck by a sense of profound awe. The Manhattan Project had unleashed the power of the atom, and the world would never be the same again.

CHAPTER 6
ETHICAL CROSSROADS

The Pacific Theater

At the time of the Trinity test, Nazi Germany had already surrendered. Europe had been taken back by Allied forces, with Italy having surrendered two years before. The only holdout was Imperialist Japan, and their eventual defeat was all but assured.

In this light, we might harshly judge Truman's decision to drop atomic bombs on Hiroshima and Nagasaki. The death toll from the atomic bombs was between 129,000 and 226,000, once we account for deaths caused by radiation, and to some extent the war was already decided.

However, it is worth being careful about wholesale condemnations of Truman's decision. The firebombing of Tokyo in March 1944 had killed an estimated 100,000 people, and the United States was firebombing hundreds of Japanese towns and cities in preparation for an invasion of the mainland (codenamed "Operation Downfall"). Meanwhile, estimated casualties for Operation Downfall were 43,000 dead and wounded American soldiers every month. A study written by William Shockley for Secretary of War Henry L. Stimson estimated that invading Japan would cost the United States somewhere between 1.7 and 4 million American casualties (including 400,000 to 800,000 fatalities), and would result in between 5 and 10 million Japanese fatalities (Frank, 1999). The deaths that might result from a conventional invasion of Japan would grossly exceed the deaths resulting from the decision to drop atomic bombs on Hiroshima and Nagasaki.

Part of the concern was the attitudes of the Japanese people. It was assumed that the Japanese population would greatly contribute to the defense of the mainland, essentially fighting to the death against an American invasion of Japan. The War Journal of the Imperial Headquarters stated in 1944 that "the only course left is for Japan's one million people to sacrifice their lives by charging the enemy to make them lose the will to fight" (quoted in Frank, 1999). Japan had already dismissed demands for its unconditional surrender from Allied forces. Moreover, its soldiers were notoriously unwilling to either be taken captive or to take military captives, instead executing American soldiers and fighting to the bitter end.

On the other hand, the moral situation is complex. The firebombing of Japan could also be considered a war crime by today's standards, and the estimates made about the casualties of Operation Downfall were just that: estimates. The likelihood—or lack thereof—of Japanese surrender was similarly based on assumptions and educated guesses rather than any clear facts. Moreover, justifying the use of atomic weapons based on comparisons between the casualties of Hiroshima and Nagasaki with Operation Downfall might rely upon a false choice. Many scientists involved in the Manhattan Project instead wanted a peaceful demonstration of the atomic bomb to intimidate Japan into surrender.

Primary among them was Leo Szilárd, a constant thorn in the side of General Groves, and architect of the Franck Report.

The Franck Report

Leo Szilárd was publicly opposed to the use of the atomic bomb in war. Despite drafting the letter to Roosevelt that Einstein signed—the letter that arguably fired the starting gun on the Manhattan Project—Szilárd would draft petitions against the bombing of Japan, hoping to reach the president with his and other scientists' concerns.

Though Szilárd was concerned with military oversight of the Manhattan Project from day one, resulting in considerable tension between himself and Groves, his most prominent opposition to the use of the atomic bomb came in July 1945, a few weeks before the Trinity test. Szilárd and other Chicago Met Lab scientists drafted the Franck Report, which advocated for a peaceful demonstration of the atomic bomb, rather than a direct military use on a civilian target.

The Franck report—signed by James Franck, Donald J. Hughes, J. J. Nickson, Eugene Rabinowitch, Glenn T. Seaborg, J. C. Stearns, and Leo Szilárd, warned about the moral and political cost for the United States in being the first to use an atomic weapon in war (Franck et al., n.d./1945):

If the United States would be the first to

release this new means of indiscriminate destruction upon mankind, she would sacrifice public support throughout the world, precipitate the race of armaments, and prejudice the possibility of reaching an international agreement on the future control of such weapons. (para 3)

In addition to advocating for a peaceful demonstration of the bomb, the Franck report also calls for international efforts to control and oversee the use of nuclear weapons.

The Franck Report was rejected by scientists on the Interim Committee's Scientific Panel, made up of Oppenheimer, Fermi, Ernest Lawrence, and Arthur Compton, who wrote that "we see no acceptable alternative to direct military use" (quoted by Atomic Heritage Foundation, 2016). However, the Franck Report was not Szilárd's only effort to prevent the military use of the atomic bomb.

Szilárd had previously presented a memo in the Spring of 1945, stating his concerns to soon-to-be-named Secretary of State, James F. Byrnes. Byrnes refused to share the memo with Truman. In response, Szilárd worked to draft a petition against the direct use of the atomic bomb, gathering signatures from scientists and technicians of the Manhattan Project. Part of the petition reads as follows (Szilárd, 1945):

The development of atomic power will provide the nations with new means of destruction. The atomic bombs at our disposal represent only the first step in this direction, and there is almost no limit to the destructive power which will become available in the course of their future development. Thus a nation which sets the precedent of using these newly liberated forces of nature for purposes of destruction may have to bear the responsibility of opening the door to an era of devastation on an unimaginable scale.

If after the war a situation is allowed to develop in the world which permits rival powers to be in uncontrolled possession of these new means of destruction, the cities of the United States as well as the cities of other nations will be in continuous danger of sudden annihilation. All the resources of the United States, moral and material, may have to be mobilized to prevent the advent of such a world situation. Its prevention is at present the solemn responsibility of the United States—singled out by virtue of her lead in the field of atomic power.

The added material strength which this lead gives to the United States brings with it the obligation of restraint and if we were to violate this obligation our moral position would be weakened in the eyes of the world and in our own eyes. It would then be more difficult for us to live up to our responsibility of bringing the unloosened forces of destruction under control. (para 5-7)

Over several drafts, the petition was signed by between 65 and 100 people at the Chicago Met Lab and Oak Ridge, despite its distribution being shut down at Oak Ridge by military authorities. The official reason for this shutdown was security, with military authorities arguing that the petition posed a security risk: given it implied that the United States had a usable atomic bomb. The petition did even worse at Los Alamos. It was brought to the site by Teller, but Oppenheimer talked him out of distributing it, making the argument that it was the job of policymakers, not scientists, to decide how the bomb would be used.

More generally, the demand for compartmentalization was a constant limitation on the petition's distribution, reducing the number of people who could sign it. After all, many people working on the Manhattan Project did not even know that they were working on an atomic bomb.

Szilárd's petition also faced direct opposition

from Groves himself, who already did not like Szilárd for his stated dislike of military oversight. Szilárd wanted the petition to reach President Truman directly, but Groves prevented that outright, insisting that the petition would follow the official chain of command. Szilárd passed the petition to Arthur Compton, who passed it to Kenneth Nichols, who then passed it to Groves. From there, Groves sent the petition to Secretary of War Henry Stimson, but not until August 1945. By this point, Stimson and Truman were still in Europe for the Potsdam Conference. When it reached Stimson's assistant, it was filed under "Secret" and then never reached either of the two men. Soon after, the bombs were dropped on Hiroshima and Nagasaki.

Szilárd would continue his efforts to warn the world about nuclear proliferation after the war, including writing his famous Letter to Stalin in the Bulletin of Atomic Scientists in 1947, in which he begged Joseph Stalin to talk directly to the American people. He also conducted a series of interviews with the then-Soviet Premier, Nikita Khrushchev in 1959-1960, and proposed the creation of a nuclear "hotline" between Moscow and Washington. But why did Szilárd, the man who had written the letter advocating for an atomic bomb project in 1939, harbor such moral opposition to the use of a bomb he had helped create?

The answer may be relatively straightforward. Szilárd was Jewish, and in 1930 received German citizenship. When Hitler became chancellor in 1933, Szilárd urged his family and friends to flee Europe while they still could. In the years that followed, Szilárd lived in fear of the Nazis creating the atomic bomb first. On this interpretation, then, Szilárd advocated for the Manhattan Project so that the United States could get the bomb before Hitler did. However, once Germany surrendered, two months before the Trinity test, the moral justification for the Manhattan Project was greatly diminished—and, at this point, Szilárd started urging against the use of the bomb.

Groves's interpretation, however, was less charitable to Szilárd. In his interview with Groueff, the general speaks in scathing terms of Szilárd's motivations (Groves, 1965a):

I do not think there is anything moral in [Szilárd's] attitude towards the Japanese, because I never saw any signs of any great moral outlook on his part. I am sure that it was just a case of, Hitler surrendered, that revenge on the Germans. After he surrendered, it was a case of, 'Well, let's do something that will make a name for myself.' (para 33)

On the other hand, it certainly seems as though Groves despised Szilárd. After the war, Groves attempted to find evidence of wrongdoing on the part of Szilárd, including writing to Churchill's scientific advisor, Frederick Lindemann, to establish whether Szilárd had mentioned classified information to him and thus broken the Espionage Act. Given that Groves's efforts were unsuccessful—Szilárd was never convicted or formally accused of any such wrongdoing—we might conclude that Groves was seeking to punish Szilárd based on a somewhat nasty vendetta. As it was, many lower-level staff on the Manhattan Project did face consequences for signing Szilárd's petition, being stripped of necessary security clearance to continue working in the weapons industry after the war.

Other Moral Qualms

Though Szilárd was the most active and vocal opponent of the use of the bomb against Japan on the Manhattan Project, this is not to say that other scientists on the project did not think about the ethical implications of the atomic bomb.

Other scientists of the Manhattan Project, including Bohr and Oppenheimer, would later become advocates for the peaceful use of nuclear power. Bohr would write his 1950 Open Letter to the United Nations, expressing his hope that "the very novelty of the situation should offer a unique opportunity" for peace and international cooperation. Oppenheimer would similarly advocate for the international control of nuclear power.

In addition, in the years following the war, a group of Manhattan Project scientists founded the Federation of American Scientists and the Bulletin of the Atomic Scientists. You will probably know of the Bulletin of the Atomic Scientists, even if you are unfamiliar with their name: The group became famous for their use of the Doomsday Clock, which tracked how close humanity is to nuclear armageddon.

However, there is no denying that many of these objections and moral qualms were only voiced after the war. Oppenheimer and Fermi were on the committee that rejected the Franck Report and acted as advisers in the selection of targets for atomic weapons. Oppenheimer further advised the American Air Force on the best height to detonate the atomic bomb to cause maximum damage to Japanese houses. Only one scientist quit the Manhattan Project on moral grounds—Joseph Rotblat, who left in late 1944, once it became clear that the Nazis were not close to developing atomic weaponry of their own. Though between 65 and 100 scientists and technicians signed Szilárd's petition—and perhaps more would have if not for the pressures of compartmentalization—the prevailing attitude among scientists of the Manhattan Project seems to have been that it was simply not the place of scientists to question how the bomb would be used. Oppenheimer, in particular, was of the view that the use of the bomb had to be decided by democratically elected officials, rather than decided by the scientists that developed the technology.

Others took an even more pragmatic approach. Teller, for instance, would later note that taking moral responsibility for the use of the atomic bomb relied on "an entirely false sense of pride... you can have regrets only if you somehow imagine that on a large scale you could have changed the course of events" (Teller, 1986). In this same interview (Teller, 1986) with Sanger, Teller would use colorful language to state his irritation at such questions of guilt and regret:

> **Teller:** It is a remarkable thing. I have been asked again and again whether I have regrets.

Sanger: Right.
Teller: Will you please excuse me, but this is one of the most idiotic questions, except for the fact that apparently others do. I may suffer from some moral insufficiency, but I do not.

I did not put the work together. If you had the choice that something simply was in the long term unavoidable should be first done by the United States or by the Nazis or by the Soviets or by someone else, would you have regrets to make sure that we did it first?

Sanger: No.
Teller: And I do not. (para 85-90)

And yet, Teller was the man who brought Szilárd's petition to Los Alamos, before Oppenheimer talked him out of distributing it. Perhaps the truth is that many of the scientists and technicians working on the Manhattan Project were conflicted. We can hardly blame them. The bombing of Hiroshima and Nagasaki remains morally controversial. According to some, it saved lives. According to others, it was a moral atrocity.

Perhaps, in truth, it was both—and that is the difficult fact. Either way, on August 6, 1945, the United States dropped the bomb on Hiroshima, marking the first use of an atomic weapon in war.

CHAPTER 7
UNLEASHING THE BEAST

Little Boy and Fat Man

On August 6, 1945, a gun-type atomic bomb, "Little Boy," was dropped on Hiroshima. Three days later, on August 9, an implosion-type atomic bomb, "Fat Man," was dropped on Nagasaki.

Due to the chaos of war, and the indiscriminate violence of atomic weapons, it is difficult to know precisely how many people were killed. The United States military claimed that 70,000 people had died at Hiroshima and 40,000 at Nagasaki, for a total of 110,000 people.

However, later estimates made by scientists

in the 1970s claim that 140,000 people died as a result of nuclear weapons at Hiroshima, and 70,000 at Nagasaki: for a total of 210,000 people. The gap may be partly explicable by a greater understanding of the deadly effects of radiation by the 1970s. Either way, with merely two bombs, an enormous number of people were suddenly and violently killed.

Masao Tomonaga is an honorary director of the Japanese Red Cross Nagasaki Atomic Bomb Hospital, and a hibakusha: an atomic bomb survivor. He was a child when the bomb hit Nagasaki, and survived only because he was staying home with a fever at the time of the blast.

Many buildings in Nagasaki were made of wood. The explosion of Fat Man resulted in a firestorm that claimed many of the buildings not in the immediate blast radius of the nuclear explosion. Tomonaga's mother took him out of their family home—which had been badly damaged by the shock wave—before the fires reached them, and they sheltered at a nearby shrine. Meanwhile, his father was an army doctor stationed outside the city. He thought that his family had been killed, only to discover that they had survived a month later.

Tomonaga describes the sights he saw within

one kilometer of Ground Zero. Be warned: His description is graphic, and informed by his medical understanding (Tomonaga, 2019):

The situation was terrible. Many, many carbonized bodies were seen. Also, white bones were seen. Carbonization occurred by the strong direct heat rays from the detonation. Those people walking on the street were directly exposed to heat rays. Later, the bodies were burned again by the firestorms. Then, become white ones. Some docs wrote the atomic bomb energy evaporated human bodies directly to white ones. This might not be correct in terms of the physical power of heat rays. Heat rays have not such a huge energy to make the human body evaporate, okay... Evaporation is instantaneous destruction of all organs, all deep organs, but this was not true. Maybe I suspect, that black boy, inside his body still organs are existing, but later if he was burned by fire, firestorms, his body became only white bones. (para 17)

Some people were partially caught in the blast and faced an even more nightmarish fate. Once more, be warned that the description is graphic (Tomonaga, 2019):

The skin began peeling off and bleeding and the pain. This is a terrible situation. Even the skin of [their] arms [was] hanging down. Almost all of them walked like this if they were still alive. Most of them died sooner or later. (para 24)

Dr Takashi Nagai, a Japanese physician specializing in radiology, later wrote of finding the remains of his wife in the ruin of his house. He tried to collect his wife's bones, but they disintegrated to ash when he touched them: "My wife escaped from my fingers. Escaped from my fingers" (quoted in Tomonaga, 2019).

There was no immediate medical help for the survivors of the blast. The bomb at Nagasaki killed 55% of the doctors and students in the city, and all major medical facilities—along with their medicines, drugs, and blood transfusions—had been destroyed. People with severe burns would soon die from their horrific injuries.

Next came the effects of deadly radiation poisoning. Within two weeks, survivors of the blast began to lose their hair. Babies were born with microcephaly, a condition in which they are born with smaller heads and underdeveloped brains. Adults and children alike died painful deaths from bone marrow destruction. Tomonaga describes one such case referring to a photograph of a young boy—again, in graphic terms that some readers may wish to skip

(Tomonaga, 2019):

> This is a boy agonizing and died within a few days after this photograph, showing some extraneous skin bleeding. This was a typical sign of bone marrow destruction. You know bone marrow. This is normal bone marrow. This is such a heavily irradiated people's bone marrow autopsy tissue photograph. There were no blood cells being made. So platelets, that prevent bleeding, became almost zero. Then, their capillaries and small vessels began to bleed spontaneously. So they die. Also, those photographs, again, show hair falling [out]. (para 33)

Rates of leukemia spiked in the months that followed, and the spike in the rates of throat cancer continues to this day (Tomonaga, 2019).

This was Nagasaki. Hiroshima suffered a similar fate. There were 298 physicians still in Hiroshima at the time of the bombing. 90% of these physicians were injured or killed by the atomic blast, leaving only 28 physicians who were uninjured. Black shadows of humans and objects were cast onto the sidewalk, due to the nuclear blast scorching surfaces not shielded by people and bicycles. People wearing patterned, dark clothing had the stripes of their clothing burned into their skin. At least 80,000 people died instantly.

The Selection of Hiroshima and Nagasaki

In the days and weeks before the bombing of Hiroshima and Nagasaki, there was extensive talk about which cities would be targeted, and when. The Target Committee (n.d.) identified three criteria for a viable target, such that the target should:

- be a large urban area, not less than three miles in diameter
- not already be in ruins as a result of the 20th Air Force's conventional bombing efforts
- be unlikely to be attacked before August 1946

The purpose of the criteria was to ensure that the targets of the bombings would ensure significant enough damage to maximize the psychological impact of a nuclear attack. The thought was that the only way to get Japan to surrender was to demonstrate the full, horrendous capabilities of the atomic bomb—and that this would save lives in the long run. Based on the criteria, six potential targets were identified: Kokura, Yokohama, Hiroshima, Kyoto, and Niigata.

Kyoto was later removed from consideration and replaced with Nagasaki. Secretary of War Stimson persuaded Truman that Kyoto had too great a cultural importance to be an acceptable target for an atomic bomb (Oi, 2015).

On July 25, 1945, the targets were ranked in order of highest preference to least: Hiroshima, Kokura, and Nagasaki. Hiroshima was home to the 2nd Army Headquarters of the Japanese Army, responsible for the defense of southern Japan. It was also a logistical center for the storage, communication, and assembly of soldiers. Due to the rivers running through the city, it had not been firebombed by the U.S. 20th Air Force. Moreover, its nearby hills would increase the destructive force of the atomic blast.

Kokura, meanwhile, contained the largest factory in western Japan for producing weapons, aircraft, and missiles. Finally, Nagasaki was a major military port and an important producer of naval weapons.

Another major consideration for the Target Committee was the problem of weather conditions. Based on the available weather maps, there were only an average of six days in August with weather fair enough to drop the bombs. Narrowing this down to a conservative estimate of three days, the Target Committee (n.d.) selected the window between August 6 and 9.

Hiroshima's weather report for August 6 showed a clear day, allowing plans to proceed. However, Kokura was covered by a cloud on August 9. By this quirk of fate, Nagasaki was bombed instead.

The Immediate Impact

Due to the destruction of phone lines, it took some time for military leaders in Tokyo to understand what had happened in Hiroshima. Rumors of a huge explosion reached the Imperial Japanese Army General Staff, but these came from small railway stops within ten miles of Hiroshima, and were invariably unofficial and confused. Attempts to ring the Army Control Station in Hiroshima failed, puzzling the General Staff, who knew that no sizable enemy raid had taken place and that there was no sizable store of explosives in Hiroshima at that time. A young officer was ordered to fly immediately to Hiroshima to find out what was going on. At the time, personnel in Tokyo did not think that anything serious had taken place.

After flying for three hours, still nearly 100 miles from Hiroshima, the officer and his pilot saw a great cloud of smoke rising from Hiroshima. He reported to Tokyo and the Japanese government began to organize relief measures.

Despite this, the Army General Staff still did not truly know what had happened until Truman announced the bombing, sixteen hours after the blast. In Truman's speech, which was widely broadcast across Japan, he warned that Japan must unconditionally surrender at once (Truman, 1945):

We are now prepared to obliterate more rapidly and completely every productive enterprise the Japanese have above ground in any city. We shall destroy their docks, their factories, and their communications. Let there be no mistake; we shall completely destroy Japan's power to make war.

It was to spare the Japanese people from utter destruction that the ultimatum of July 26 was issued at Potsdam. Their leaders promptly rejected that ultimatum. If they do not now accept our terms they may expect a rain of ruin from the air, the like of which has never been seen on this earth. Behind this air attack will follow sea and land forces in such number and power as they have not yet seen and with the fighting skill of which they are already well aware. (para 9-10)

Despite these warnings, Japan did not surrender. Admiral Soemu Toyoda, the Chief of the Imperial Japanese Naval General Staff, estimated that the United States was unlikely to have more than two additional bombs, and advised that "there would be more destruction but the war would go on" (quoted in Hoyt, 2001). Meanwhile, the leadership of the Japanese Army started preparations to impose martial law on Japan, the measure supported by Minister of War Korechicka Anami, to prevent anyone from attempting to make peace with the Allies. All these messages were intercepted by American codebreakers, and the decision was made to drop the second bomb.

There were plans for further atomic attacks should Japan not surrender after Nagasaki. Groves expected to have another implosion-type atomic bomb ready for use on August 19, with three more in September and another three in October. As it was, Emperor Hirohito issued Japan's declaration of surrender on August 15 on only one condition: that kokutai, or the sovereignty of the Emperor, would be preserved. In his declaration, the Emperor directly alluded to the use of nuclear weapons (1945):

Moreover, the enemy has begun to employ a new and most cruel bomb, the power of which to do damage is, indeed, incalculable, taking the toll of many innocent lives. Should we continue to fight, not only would it result in an ultimate collapse and obliteration of the Japanese nation, but also it would lead to the total extinction of human civilization. (para 6)

With the surrender of Japan, the Second World War was over.

The immediate impact of Hiroshima and Nagasaki was also felt in Soviet Russia. Despite the warnings from the Soviet spy on the Manhattan Project, Klaus Fuchs, Stalin did not fully appreciate the military capacity of atomic weapons until they were used. According to a New York Times review of historian David Holloway's 1994 Stalin and the Bomb (McMillan, 1994), "after the bomb was dropped, Stalin was furious. The place Russia had earned as a world power by its victory in the war had been snatched away. 'Hiroshima has shaken the whole world,' he is said to have told Kurchatov. 'The balance has been destroyed.'"

Back in the United States, there was jubilation and celebration. In Hanford, Oak Ridge, and Los Alamos, many Manhattan Project personnel were only just then discovering what they had been working on for the last four years. With the end of the Second World War, American soldiers could return home, safe and sound, to their families and loved ones. Philip S. Anderson Jr., who had lived as a boy at Oak Ridge, later reflected on the sense of pride he felt when he learned what the site had been working on: "At last, we knew what we were doing here, and we were very proud of the fact that we were. We knew that they dropped one bomb and then dropped another bomb and it was all over, the war was over" (Anderson, 2018).

Long-Term Consequences

One of the most direct long-term consequences of the bombings of Hiroshima and Nagasaki was the start of a nuclear arms race between the United States and the Soviet Union. The atomic age had begun, and Stalin now wrote a blank check for his scientists to make a Soviet atomic weapon. In the next chapter, we will focus on this arms race and the backdrop of the Cold War in which it took place.

In addition to the rising tensions between the United States and the Soviet Union, the use of atomic weapons had a terrible impact on the survivors of Hiroshima and Nagasaki. We have already spoken of the spiked rates of leukemia and other cancers. The Radiation Effects Research Foundation (Listwa, 2012) estimates that bomb victims were 46% more likely to develop leukemia, mostly affecting children. The peak in the rate of leukemia took place four to six years after the bombings—a bitter, lasting impact of the atomic weapons.

Meanwhile, spikes in other cancers were not evident until around ten years after the attacks. A team led by Dale L. Preston of the Hirosoft International Corporation (2003) estimated that people exposed to the bomb were 10.7% more likely to develop cancer other than leukemia, primarily throat cancer.

There are few silver linings in this bleak medical story. However, we can take some small comfort in the fact that there does not seem to be any medical impact on children conceived after the bombings. Dan Listwa of the Columbia K=1 Project (2012) notes that "though more time is needed to be able to know for certain," there does not seem to be a higher incidence of radiation-related diseases among the more recently born populations of Hiroshima and Nagasaki. Additionally, Hiroshima and Nagasaki are not themselves radioactive, and have been rebuilt: A tribute to the human spirit, and our capacity to rebuild that which was destroyed.

The bombings of Hiroshima and Nagasaki remain the only two military uses of atomic weapons in human history. Though we have come close to nuclear disaster over the years, and geopolitics are as fraught today as ever, we must hope that this trend continues: for the good of humankind and our struggling world.

The final lasting impact of the use of atomic weapons is on the reputation of the United States. A common refrain among America's opponents is that it is in no position to insist on moral superiority since it is the only country to have used atomic weapons on another. We can only guess at how this has, directly and indirectly, impacted the United States' ability to influence political events across the world, and what cost the United States has paid for its decision to bomb Hiroshima and Nagasaki.

CHAPTER 8
COLD WAR AND ARMS RACE

Stalin and Truman

Between July 17 and August 2, 1945, Winston Churchill, Joseph Stalin, and Harry Truman met for the Potsdam Conference, named for the German town in which the conference was held. Germany had surrendered, and the "Big Three" were meeting to discuss the future of Europe and, indeed, the world.

The successful Trinity test had taken place just one day before the conference, on July 16, 1945. Truman came to the conference with the confidence of a man with an ace in his back pocket. Moreover, he had something to prove.

The Potsdam Conference was Truman's first major appearance on the world stage, after Roosevelt's death on April 12 of the same year.

The conference had its moments of tension. Given that Germany had surrendered, the Soviet Union was no longer at war, having not yet declared war on Imperial Japan. Meanwhile, Stalin wanted to extract huge reparations from Germany for the damage it had dealt to the Soviet Union—an aim that Roosevelt had previously tolerated in his efforts to bring the Soviet Union into the war against Japan. Truman, meanwhile, was in less of a compromising mood. He feared that huge reparations would result in another Treaty of Versailles—a treaty that severely penalized Germany after the First World War, and arguably contributed to the economic and political conditions that allowed Hitler to rise to power.

Despite the difficult challenges of the Potsdam Conference, Truman seemed to like Stalin. In a letter to his wife, written on July 29, 1945, he wrote "I like Stalin... he is straightforward, knows what he wants and will compromise when he can't get it" (quoted by Phillips, 2018). But it is not clear whether the feeling was mutual. When the bomb was dropped on Hiroshima, Stalin seemed displeased that Truman, "that noisy shopkeeper" (quoted in McMillan, 1994), had the bomb while he did not.

Regardless of the personal relationship between the two men, they certainly had very different political views. As they carved up Europe and Berlin between the East and West, Stalin alarmed the United States by refusing to promise free and fair elections in Eastern Europe after the war. Moreover, the Soviet Union and the United States had entirely different political and economic systems. The former was communist, the latter capitalist. Though they may have been allies in the Second World War, the two countries were powerful rivals, and tensions were all but inevitable.

The United States feared that Stalin was attempting to expand communism across Europe. In 1946, the Iron Curtain fell across Europe, sharply delineating the East and West, and the control of Soviet Russia over the former. The following year, in 1947, the United States officially adopted a policy of containment to restrict the USSR's expansion. The so-called "Truman Doctrine" was outlined in an eighteen-minute speech to Congress on March 12, 1947, and offered "an open promise of U.S. support to any country threatened by the Soviet Union" (Burton, n.d.). The North Atlantic Treaty Organization (NATO) was formed in 1949, a defensive military alliance between Western European nations further designed to curb Soviet expansion. Battlelines were being drawn, and tensions between the East and West were rising—many of which are still felt to this day.

The Downfall of Oppenheimer

In the 1930s and early 1940s, to be a communist was an eccentricity, but not something to be considered a permanent black mark against your character. The Great Depression drove many people's sympathies to the left, and little was known of the Great Purge taking place in Soviet Russia under Stalin's brutal regime. Moreover, toward the end of the Second World War, the Soviets were military allies of the United States. Soviet Russia had been devastated by the war against the Nazis, losing 8.7 million of its military and 19 million civilians. This was by far the highest casualty rate of any country in the Second World War— to put it into context, the German military lost 5.3 million soldiers and they lost the war. In addition to these appalling casualties, the conflict on the Eastern Front ravaged western Russia. Though the FBI and military police were concerned about communism, a general fear of the "Reds" had not yet reached the general population of the United States.

By 1954, that had all changed. The Cold War was in full swing. On August 29, 1949, the Soviets successfully detonated their own atomic bomb, called RDS-1 or "First Lightning." America was no longer the only nation with atomic weapons.

Additionally, the United States had just had its first taste of war against communist forces. The Korean War, a brutal three-year conflict that led to the deaths of three million people, started on June 25, 1950, and ended on July 27, 1953, with the signing of an armistice that has kept the peninsula divided to this day. North Korea was supported by the Soviet Union, and South Korea was supported by the United States.

In this context, Republican Senator Joseph McCarthy's "Red Scare" reached a fever pitch. In 1953, McCarthy made clear his position (quoted by the Miller Center, n.d.):

Any man who has been named by either a senator or a committee or a congressman as dangerous to the welfare of this nation, his name should be submitted to the various intelligence units, and they should conduct a complete check upon him. It's not too much to ask. (para 2)

Oppenheimer, by this time, had made numerous enemies in Washington. In particular, he had earned the enmity of the commissioner for the Atomic Energy Commission (AEC): Lewis Strauss. Oppenheimer had publicly mocked Strauss' security concerns about the exporting of radioactive isotopes and was an outspoken liberal whereas Strauss was a staunch conservative. Oppenheimer had become a thorn in the side of government agencies by advocating against proliferation and warning about the capability of atomic weapons to destroy human civilization. Moreover, Oppenheimer was ardently opposed to the creation of the hydrogen bomb, butting heads with Strauss, who supported the development of the bomb. Oppenheimer had made himself a target of the establishment, and the establishment would take him down.

The hydrogen bomb, known as the "H-bomb" or the "Super," boasted a destructive power far exceeding that of the atomic bomb. Oppenheimer was morally opposed to its development, arguing that there was no legitimate target for such a destructive weapon and that the H-bomb amounted to a weapon of genocide. Additionally, he was dubious of the feasibility of the H-bomb project. The AEC's General Advisory Committee (headed by Oppenheimer) had unanimously recommended that the H-bomb program remain at a theoretical level only, on the basis that manufacturing such a weapon was not technically possible at that time. As it was, Truman had overruled the committee in 1950, and the development of the H-bomb had begun under the auspices of Teller.

Furthermore, Oppenheimer's past made him an easy target. His brother Frank had been a member of the Communist Party. His lover, Jean Tatlock, had been a communist. His wife, Katherine "Kitty" Oppenheimer, also had historical ties to the Communist Party. Many of his students and colleagues were communists or unionists. Oppenheimer had donated funds to communist projects, including the funding of ambulances in the Spanish Civil War. Oppenheimer, though not a member of the Communist Party, had attended communist meetings. These facts may not have been entirely damning in the early 1940s (though, it should be noted, they were seen as problematic), but, in the Red Scare of the 1950s, such associations were enough to end careers.

Finally, there was the Chevalier incident. In August 1943, Oppenheimer told an agent of the Counter Intelligence Corps (CIC) that the Russians had attempted to gather information about the Manhattan Project, asserting that an acquaintance, George Elenton, had asked a third party to contact scientists at Los Alamos (Nichols, 1954). Oppenheimer was reluctant to tell the CIC who this third party was, but, under orders from Groves, later revealed it to be his friend, Haakon Chevalier, a professor of French Literature. Oppenheimer later recanted the entire story, but by that point, he had given many vague and conflicting accounts of the events. This deeply concerned the CIC and added a further black mark against Oppenheimer's name.

The U.S. government security hearings on Oppenheimer began in late 1953. William L. Borden, the former executive director of the Joint Congressional Committee on Atomic Energy, denounced Oppenheimer to J. Edgar Hoover, Director of the FBI, in an unsolicited letter. Hoover contacted Dwight D. Eisenhower, who by now was President of the United States, and Eisenhower ordered that a "blank wall be placed" between Oppenheimer and any secret data, pending a security hearing (The New York Times, 1967).

With the enemies Oppenheimer had made among the establishment, the security hearing was more a kangaroo court than an administrative panel. Because it was not officially a trial, there were no laws of evidence to be observed. Evidence was brought against Oppenheimer that neither he nor his lawyer had the security clearance to access or cross-examine, while the lawyer leading the case against him—Roger Robb, a prosecutor in all but name—had complete clearance. The security services had been wiretapping and following Oppenheimer for years, from before he was even involved in the Manhattan Project. The case was decided before it began, and the Personnel Security Board of the AEC declined to reinstate Oppenheimer's security clearance by a vote of two to one (Nichols, 1954). Oppenheimer appealed the decision, but lost at appeal, four to one.

In its obituary for Oppenheimer, the New York Times (1967) notes that the action against Oppenheimer "dismayed the scientific community and many other Americans. He was widely pictured as a victim of McCarthyism who was being penalized for holding honest, if unpopular, opinions."

Most of the scientists brought in as witnesses

in the trial against Oppenheimer supported their former colleague. A characteristic example of this support came from Bethe. When asked about Oppenheimer's loyalty, he replied as follows (Atomic Archives, 2006/1954):

I have absolute faith in Dr. Oppenheimer's loyalty. I have always found that he had the best interests of the United States at heart. I have always found that if he differed from other people in his judgment, that it was because of a deeper thinking about the possible consequences of our action than the other people had. I believe that it is an expression of loyalty—of particular loyalty—if a person tries to go beyond the obvious and tries to make available his deeper insight, even in making unpopular suggestions, even in making suggestions which are not the obvious ones to make, are not those which a normal intellect might be led to make.

I have absolutely no question that he has served this country very long and very well. I think everybody agrees that his service in Los Alamos was one of the greatest services that were given to this country. I believe he has served equally well in the GAC in reestablishing the strength of our atomic weapons program in 1947. I have faith in him quite generally. (para

21-22)

However, not all scientists supported Oppenheimer. Teller, father of the hydrogen bomb, infamously testified against his former colleague (quoted in the New York Times, 1967):

In a great number of cases I have seen Dr. Oppenheimer act—I understood that Dr. Oppenheimer acted—in a way which for me was exceedingly hard to understand. I thoroughly disagreed with him in numerous issues and his actions frankly appeared to me confused and complicated. To this extent I feel that I would like to see the vital interests of this country in hands which I understand better, and therefore trust more.

In this very limited sense I would like to express a feeling that I would personally feel more secure if public matters would rest in other hands.

We can only speculate why Teller was inclined to testify against Oppenheimer. Perhaps he still held a grudge for being passed up for Head of the Theoretical Division at Los Alamos. Perhaps he was frustrated by Oppenheimer's opposition to the hydrogen bomb project: A project that was headed by Teller himself. Jogalekar (2014) argues that

Teller had "let personal feelings interfere with objective decision making."

Either way, Teller would later attempt to downplay both his involvement in the hydrogen bomb and the downfall of Oppenheimer, stating that had he done nothing, the H-bomb would still have been developed, and Oppenheimer would still have lost his security clearance. Nonetheless, Teller paid a personal price for what many physicists saw as his betrayal. Jogalekar (2014) writes that "close friends simply stopped talking to him and one former colleague publicly refused to shake his hand, a defiant display that led Teller to retire to his room and weep."

Oppenheimer no longer had security clearance to work on the AEC. He kept his position at Princeton, but he no longer had much in the way of political influence over American atomic policy. However, his reputation was later somewhat restored in December 1963. Then-President Kennedy awarded Oppenheimer with the Fermi Award, a tax-free $50,000 prize that was the highest award of the AEC. Oppenheimer would die of throat cancer four years later—no doubt a consequence of his chain smoking and extensive work with radioactive materials at Los Alamos.

On December 16, 2022, the decision to remove Oppenheimer's clearance was vacated by the U.S. Secretary of the Department of Energy, Jennifer Granholm. In her statement, she wrote that Oppenheimer's clearance was revoked "through a flawed process that violated the Commission's regulations. As time has passed, more evidence has come to light of the bias and unfairness of the process that Dr. Oppenheimer was subjected to while the evidence of his loyalty and love of country have only been further affirmed" (Granholm, 2022).

The Arms Race

In the 1950s, McCarthyism was at its peak. The Red Scare had swept across the United States. A war had been fought in Korea. The Iron Curtain had been drawn across Europe. The Vietnam War had begun on November 1, 1955, drawing the United States into another war against communism, this time a conflict that would last twenty years and cost millions of lives. On August 13, 1961, the Berlin Wall was completed, separating families and preventing access from one side of Berlin to the other. The Cold War was in full effect.

However, with the advent of the atomic age, the world was changed. Despite tensions between the United States and the Soviet Union, there was never an outright war between the two nations. Such a war would violate the principle of Mutually Assured Destruction (MAD): The principle that if one nuclear power attacked another nuclear power, both sides would be utterly destroyed (as well as, quite possibly, the entire world). However, this principle was constantly being challenged through an ongoing arms race, and the development of new weapons of mass destruction.

On November 1, 1952, the first thermonuclear weapon (that is, hydrogen bomb) was successfully tested at Enewetak Atoll in the Marshall Islands. Once again, America had gotten there first, but the Soviet hydrogen bomb was not far behind, first successfully tested on November 22, 1955. Both countries continued to develop nuclear weapons and build up their arsenal, seeking a geopolitical advantage until they could destroy the world many times over. It is estimated that at the time of the Soviet Union's collapse, it had approximately 40,000 nuclear weapons, while the United States had around 30,000 at its peak in 1967 (Aljazeera, 2023) Between 1940 and 1996, the United States spent roughly $5.5 trillion on its nuclear weapons program—11% of all Federal Government spending. Meanwhile, estimates of Soviet expenditure on its nuclear weapons program suggest that 35% of its Gross Domestic Product (GDP) was spent on the development and maintenance of Soviet nuclear weapons: certainly enough to contribute to the USSR's economic collapse in 1991.

We might wonder why hydrogen bombs were necessary. Atomic bombs already had a vast destructive power, enough to devastate entire cities like New York and Moscow. Hydrogen bombs were greatly more powerful—the bomb at Trinity had a yield of 25 kilotons at TNT, while the first hydrogen bomb had a yield of 10.4 megatons, 500 times larger—but we might ask why this mattered, given the potential for destruction offered by atomic weaponry. However, according to Teller, this is to miss the point. In an interview recorded at the NS Archive (n.d.), Teller notes that the real advantage of the H-bomb was not its increased destructive force, but its flexibility and cost. The H-bomb was much easier and cheaper to manufacture, and the size of the explosion could be tailored by the amount of deuterium (an isotope of hydrogen) used in the bomb. The development of thermonuclear bombs allowed for a much larger stockpile of weapons to be built up more quickly and for less cost.

And yet, we might still raise doubts. Why did

the United States and the Soviet Union need stockpiles big enough to destroy the world several times over? Did the brinkmanship of mutually assured destruction save lives, or risk them unnecessarily? Have thermonuclear weapons been a force for peace, or have they contributed to geopolitical conflicts and tensions?

Such questions are not easy to answer.

CHAPTER 9
LEGACY AND LESSONS

Putting the Genie Back in the Bottle
Some scientists on the Manhattan Project, most notably Leo Szilárd, attempted to prevent the military use of the atomic bomb. Others set up committees or otherwise devoted political efforts to limiting proliferation after the war, including Oppenheimer, Bohr, and Bethe. None of these efforts, no matter how earnest or genuine, were successful in putting the genie back in the bottle. There was a significant proliferation of atomic and thermonuclear weapons in the last half of the twentieth century, and thermonuclear arsenals exist to this day.

A notable attempt to advocate for the

abolition of thermonuclear weapons came on July 9, 1955, in the form of the Russell-Einstein Manifesto. Named for British mathematician and philosopher Bertrand Russell (as well as, of course, the famous physicist Albert Einstein), the manifesto was signed by various scientists, including Max Born. Presented in the heart of the Cold War, it urges for the peoples of the world to set aside their political differences, and to "consider yourselves only as members of a biological species which has had a remarkable history, and whose disappearance none of us can desire" (Born et al., 1955). Moreover, the manifesto gives a grim warning about what is at stake, noting that a thermonuclear war "might quite possible put an end to the human race... there will be universal death—sudden only for a minority, but for the majority a slow torture of disease and disintegration" (Born et al., 1955)

Chairman of the Nobel Committee, Gunnar Jahn would later quote Einstein when awarding scientist Linus Carl Pauling with the Nobel Peace Prize for his efforts in opposing nuclear proliferation (Jahn, 1962):

The time has come now, when man must give up war. It is no longer rational to solve international problems by resorting to war. Now that an atomic bomb, such as the bombs exploded at Hiroshima and Nagasaki, can destroy a city, kill all the people in a city, a small city the size of Minneapolis, say, we can see that we must now make use of man's powers of reason, in order to settle disputes between nations.

In accordance with the principles of justice we must develop international law, strengthen the United Nations, and have peace in the world from now on. (para 2-3)

Like many political efforts made by academics and scientists in the wake of the Manhattan Project, neither the Russell-Einstein Manifesto nor Einstein's efforts seemed to have much influence on nuclear policymaking, either in the United States or in Soviet Russia. As noted in the previous chapter, the arms race for thermonuclear weapons led to stockpiles of weapons well above what would be required to destroy the world several times over. And yet, the Soviet Union collapsed. Its economy could not sustain itself, partly due to the tremendous expense of its nuclear projects. The Cold War ended, and the immediate threat of nuclear holocaust became a fraction more remote.

The nuclear arsenals of the United States and Russia are now a fraction of what they were at the height of the Cold War, with some steps made toward partial nuclear disarmament. According to official reports, there are just over 12,500 nuclear warheads extant in the world, with approximately 2,900 of these awaiting dismantlement as of June 2023 (Arms Control Association, 2023). This is less than a third of the number of nuclear weapons that the Soviet Union possessed at its height. However, a few sobering facts should be remembered. Nowadays, nuclear weapons do not require bombers or aircraft and can be fired by guided, ballistic missiles. Moreover, nine countries now have access to nuclear weapons, listed below alphabetically with official details of their stockpiles (Arms Control Association, 2023):

- China: 410
- France: 290
- India: 164
- Israel: 90
- North Korea: 30
- Pakistan: 170
- Russia: 5,889
- United Kingdom: 225
- United States: 5,244

Two of these countries, India and Pakistan, have been at war numerous times in the last half of the twentieth century, and to this day regularly exchange fire across their contested border, despite a 2003 ceasefire. Both countries, along with Israel, never signed the nuclear Nonproliferation Treaty (NPT) in 1968. Meanwhile, North Korea is a rogue state with an unpredictable, tyrannical leader in the form of Kim Jong Un, which withdrew from the NPT in January 2003. And Putin's Russia is as confrontational as ever, currently engaged in an illegal war with Ukraine. On March 25, 2023, the United Nations Under-Secretary-General and High Representative for Disarmament Affairs, Izumi Nakamitsu, warned that the risk of a country using nuclear weapons is higher than at any time since the Cold War (United Nations, 2023).

Furthermore, the arms race continues, just in tangential projects. The Strategic Defense Initiative (SDI), sometimes nicknamed the "Star Wars program," continues to develop military technologies that will defend the United States against nuclear weapons. This research has cost hundreds of billions of dollars. Russia has its own anti-ballistic missile system. It is unclear whether these systems would successfully prevent a nuclear attack—and whether it is even to the benefit of humanity if they would. Should one country gain a conclusive advantage, the principle of mutually assured destruction is obliterated. And, for every technological leap in missile defense, we might worry that a counter-technological leap in nuclear weapons is only a couple of years behind.

On the other hand, Hiroshima and Nagasaki are the only two instances of atomic weapons being used as an act of war. Furthermore, thermonuclear weapons have never been used in war. Though the advent of the atomic age has not brought an end to war, it seems that the world has nonetheless managed not to destroy humanity with thermonuclear conflict. Of course, we must hope that this trend continues. For there is no putting the genie back in the bottle: Even if we achieve complete disarmament and dismantle every nuclear weapon, the knowledge of how to make another hydrogen bomb will nonetheless remain as a grim specter on the world.

The Legacy of Radiation

Hiroshima and Nagasaki have mostly recovered from the atomic bombs dropped on them in 1945. The cities have been rebuilt, radiation levels are normal, and the descendants of atomic bomb survivors show no sign of diseases related to radiation. However, the long-term effects of radiation have been felt not only in cities attacked by nuclear weapons but also downwind of sites where nuclear research was undertaken.

Curiously, Teller—the father of the hydrogen bomb—remained skeptical of the harmful effects of radiation, arguing that "the fear of radioactivity has been greatly and improperly exaggerated" (NS Archive, n.d.). When asked about the first tests of the hydrogen bomb, he notes that a Japanese fishing boat ignored American warnings to avoid the site and that one person died of radiation:

I won't say it's bad and I certainly won't say it's good, but I will say remarkable, that this one death shocked Americans more than Hiroshima. It gave rise to enormous and unjustified fears of radioactivity. No, that fear was already there, but it seemed to justify that fear. (NS Archive, n.d., para 8)

Tom Foulds is an attorney who has represented plaintiffs downwind of the Hanford Nuclear Reservation in Washington State. The Hanford site, responsible for producing plutonium during the Manhattan Project, has had a lasting impact on the health of communities downwind of its factories—despite Groves' apparent efforts in protecting the local salmon from ecological damage.

The plutonium-making process produces

various by-products, one of which is the radioactive iodine-131 gas. To prevent radiation from settling over the Hanford site, a 200-foot chimney was built to funnel away the gas and scatter it away by wind from the area. However, what was good for the scientists and technicians at Hanford was bad for communities living downwind of this chimney.

Foulds has represented several thousand plaintiffs who suffered hypothyroidism, and 300 plaintiffs who have suffered thyroid cancer. He is angry with what he sees as intentionally neglectful behavior from the site managers at Hanford (Foulds, 2019). If authorities had issued a public caution warning nearby communities to take iodine salt, exposure would have been reduced by about 80%. However, due to concerns about legal liabilities, no such caution was issued. Moreover, iodine-131 has a relatively short half-life of eight days. If the iodine-131 gas had been contained safely in the factory for just eight days, exposure would similarly have been drastically reduced.

Due to the pressures of the Manhattan Project and the Cold War, the Hanford site would regularly produce between ten and fifty curies—the official measurement of radiation—a day over a twenty-five-year period. The release of just one curie a day would have been sufficient to cause a health problem in local communities.

Additionally, despite Groves' claims about protecting the salmon, the river running through the Hanford site was also greatly exposed to radiation. Waste products found their way into the river, being absorbed by plankton and entering the food chain. This would further expose the local human populations to another source of radiation, causing cancers, birth defects, and autoimmune diseases.

Sadly, this is not simply Hanford's legacy, but the legacy of other sites involved in the Manhattan Project. Counties downwind of the Trinity test near Los Alamos suffered high rates of infant mortality, and residents of southern New Mexico continue to petition the United States government to take responsibility for this lasting damage (Cramer, 2020).

Nuclear Weapons and International Politics

The stability-instability paradox holds that when two countries have nuclear weapons, the chance of a direct war between them greatly decreases, but the chance of minor or indirect conflicts between them increases (Kapur, 2017).

The reasoning behind the stability-instability paradox is as follows. Neither side wants thermonuclear war, because of mutually assured destruction: This explains why the chance of a direct war between two nuclear-armed countries is greatly reduced. However, because of the risk of thermonuclear war and mutually assured destruction, neither country wants to escalate a minor conflict into something more serious. This acts as a green light for both countries to take part in minor or indirect conflicts because they know it is highly unlikely to lead to a direct war.

The stability-instability paradox seems confirmed by history. During the Cold War, the United States and the Soviet Union never engaged in direct warfare, but fought many proxy wars in Afghanistan, Angola, Korea, the Middle East, Nicaragua, and Vietnam, and spent vast amounts of money and time attempting to gain relative influence over the developing world. Similarly, the India-Pakistan relationship has been one of many minor wars and ceasefire violations, but never direct, thermonuclear war. A study published in the Journal of Conflict Resolution (Rauchhaus, 2009) found quantitative evidence of the paradox in action, suggesting that nuclear weapons are simultaneously a force for stability and instability in the world.

Arguably, we see the stability-instability paradox at work between modern Russia and the countries of NATO. The war in Ukraine is not a direct war between Russia and NATO, but NATO countries have contributed to Ukraine's defense against Russia in the form of military equipment and funds. To some extent, the illegal invasion of Ukraine can be considered an indirect, proxy war between Russia and the United States.

When viewed in this light, the legacy of nuclear weapons on international politics is complex. There is evidence that they have prevented catastrophic, direct war between powerful countries, such as the United States and Russia. However, they have also contributed to the proliferation of minor conflicts that have a very real cost in lives, property damage, and ecological disaster. As of August 18, 2023, United States officials have estimated that "the total number of Ukrainian and Russian troops killed or wounded since the war in Ukraine... is nearing 500,000" (Cooper, Gibbons-Neff, Schmitt & Barnes, 2023), a figure that does include civilian casualties of the war. In eighteen months, the death toll of the Ukraine war is already higher than the number of those killed at Hiroshima and Nagasaki combined. On the other hand, perhaps the proliferation of nuclear weapons has prevented conflicts that would have had a much greater death toll. Ultimately, we can only speculate one way or another.

In the same interview in which Teller downplayed the impact of radiation, he criticized the idea of nuclear disarmament as the "superstition [that] the less weapons, the less danger" (NS Archive, n.d.). This seems to be the opinion of contemporary military authorities, despite the misgivings of many of Teller's colleagues in the scientific community. In light of the stability-instability paradox, it might be that neither position is wholly right, or wholly wrong.

Efforts at Disarmament

The first serious efforts at disarmament came from the Japanese people, in protests against the American tests of nuclear weapons on Pacific islands. An estimated 35 million signatures were gathered in petitions calling for bans on nuclear weapons. These movements were mirrored in other countries around the world, such as the 1958 Aldermaston March in the United Kingdom, and the Women Strike for Peace on November 1, 1961, in sixty cities across the United States.

However, disarmament only became an ambition of governments later. The Nuclear Non-Proliferation Treaty (NPT) was signed in 1968, coming into force in 1970. The treaty aimed to reduce the spread of nuclear weapons, tackling the huge issues of nonproliferation, disarmament, and the right of member countries to peacefully use nuclear technology for energy. In 1995, the NPT was extended indefinitely, and 190 countries have signed on to the treaty, including China, Russia, and the United States. Only five countries have not currently signed on to the treaty as of August 2023: India, Israel, North Korea, Pakistan, and South Sudan.

The road to nonproliferation, however, has been a fraught one, requiring global consensus in a time of extraordinary global tensions. In the 1980s, President Ronald Reagan stated that he hoped to see a world without nuclear weapons, further adding to his wife Nancy that he thought the weapon was "totally irrational, totally inhumane, good for nothing but killing, possibly destructive of life on earth and civilization" (quoted by Krieger, 2008). Mikhail Gorbachev, the then-premier of the Soviet Union, seemed to share in this view, and at Reykjavik, in 1986, the two men "initiated steps leading to significant reductions in deployed long- and intermediate-range nuclear forces, including the elimination of an entire class of threatening missiles" (Schultz, Perry, Kissinger & Nunn, 2007).

There have been many additional treaties designed to counter the proliferation of nuclear weapons, and to begin the process of dismantling nuclear weapons that already exist. The United Nations supports nuclear disarmament and non-proliferation, and neither the United States nor Russia have tested a nuclear weapon since 1992. However, only one country—South Africa—has ever been known to completely disarm its nuclear arsenal, having produced six crude fission weapons in the 1980s, and later dismantled them in the early 1990s.

Moreover, nuclear disarmament remains controversial. Though nuclear weapons properly hold a horror to the peoples of the world, some critics note that the disarmament of nuclear weapons would make conventional wars more common. In light of the previous section's discussion of the stability-instability paradox, it remains unclear whether the world is better or worse off with nuclear weapons. Ultimately, reasonable people can disagree.

CHAPTER 10
NUCLEAR POWER AND FUTURE CHALLENGES

Nuclear Energy

An atomic bomb works by putting subatomic particles in a supercritical state, causing a chain reaction of fission in which atoms split. Each time an atom splits, it releases energy in the form of heat and radiation, and so this chain reaction produces a huge amount of energy that is released as a nuclear explosion. Einstein's equation: $E = mc^2$, establishes that the amount of energy that can be released from a tiny amount of matter is vast. From mere atoms, entire cities can be destroyed.

A similar procedure, however, can be used to

produce energy for our cars and homes. A nuclear reactor works a bit like a nuclear bomb but is built to avoid an uncontrolled chain reaction. Fission chain reactions can be controlled by adding or removing materials to the chain, allowing for energy to be released and harnessed safely. As of May 2023, nuclear energy provides 10% of the world's electricity from approximately 440 power reactors (World Nuclear Association, 2023).

There are significant advantages to nuclear energy. The main benefit is that it is a means of providing energy that does not release carbon dioxide or other greenhouse gasses into the atmosphere. Nuclear power plants do not pollute the air, can be built in both urban and rural areas, and do not have a disastrous ecological impact on their surroundings. They are a source of clean, reliable energy.

However, there are disadvantages, too. Though nuclear energy does not produce greenhouse gasses as a byproduct, it does produce radioactive material—a collection of unstable atomic nuclei. As these nuclei lose their energy, they can cause radiation damage to other materials in the vicinity. If this radioactive material is not properly dealt with, this can cause ecological and health disasters such as cancers, birth defects, and immune disorders.

The current strategy for dealing with radioactive waste is to store it out of the way. The final resting home of most radioactive waste is deep under the ground, in lead containers that act as a shield against radiation. However, this can be costly, and it often proves controversial where radioactive waste should be kept. Though the safe disposal of radioactive waste should not result in any health or ecological complications to the nearby area, the waste can remain reactive for hundreds of thousands of years, and local communities are often worried about what might go wrong over such a length of time.

Another downside of nuclear energy is the upfront expense. The cost to build a nuclear power plant is expensive when compared with coal-based power plants, and much more expensive when compared with gas-based power plants. Though nuclear power plants are much cheaper to run and maintain than these rival sources of energy, the high start-up costs provide another obstacle to the expansion of nuclear energy across the United States and abroad.

Finally, a major disadvantage of nuclear energy is its association with nuclear weapons. Because nuclear reactors require uranium-

235—a controlled substance under international law—only countries that are part of the Nuclear Non-Proliferation Treaty (NPT) can legally import material necessary to produce nuclear energy. Additionally, the association between nuclear energy and nuclear weapons leads communities to oppose the construction of new nuclear power plants, on the suspicion that they will be dangerous to local populations. Though nuclear power plants are much cleaner than coal or gas-based power plants, they are politically unpopular, making it difficult for governments to build more of them.

The Chernobyl and Fukushima Disasters

Of course, concerns about the safety of nuclear power plants are not simply the result of an association between nuclear energy and nuclear weapons. Nuclear power plants have suffered disasters in the past. The most infamous of these disasters took place at Chernobyl.

The 1986 Chernobyl disaster was not a nuclear explosion, nor an uncontrolled fission chain reaction. Instead, the reactor at Chernobyl 4 exploded due to a build-up of pressure caused by a test of its turbines. The test was to determine how long the turbines at Chernobyl 4 would spin and supply power to the pumps after a shutdown of the main power supply to the plant. As part of these tests, automatic shutdown mechanisms were disabled.

A full discussion of what happened at Chernobyl would merit its own book. Suffice it to say: A combination of human error and poor safety design caused two explosions in the reactor. Water coolant interacted with very hot fuel, causing a huge spike in pressure from steam that led the reactor to explode. This released fission products into the atmosphere and caused fires that further released elements of the radioactive reactor core into the environment. Two workers at the Chernobyl plant were killed by these explosions, and a further twenty-eight people died within a few weeks due to acute radiation syndrome. 350,000 people were evacuated, and at least 5% of the radioactive reactor core was released into the air, falling mostly on Belarus but spreading across much of Europe.

Despite these grim facts, the number of deaths attributed to the Chernobyl disaster is smaller than many people suppose. Approximately 5,000 incidents of thyroid cancer have been attributed to the incident, resulting in 15 fatalities. The United Nations

Scientific Committee on the Effects of Atomic Radiation (UNSCEAR) concluded that, aside from these incidents of thyroid cancer, "there is no evidence of a major public health impact attributable to radiation exposure 20 years after the accident" (UNSCEAR & Balanov, 2011). However, the cost in public opinion against nuclear energy was profound.

In addition to the disaster at Chernobyl, the disaster at the Fukushima nuclear power plant has contributed to a lasting suspicion of nuclear energy. The accident was caused by the Tōhoku earthquake and tsunami on March 11, 2011. This turned off both the electrical grid in Fukushima, as well as caused the failure of emergency generators at the plant, therefore disabling the pumps responsible for circulating coolant through the cores of the Fukushima reactors. Without this reactor core cooling, there were three nuclear meltdowns (in which the core overheats), three hydrogen explosions, and the release of radioactive material into the surrounding areas.

Again, though the event was serious, resulting in tens of thousands of evacuations, very few deaths have been attributed to the Fukushima disaster. There has only been one reported death—a worker who died from lung cancer attributed to radiation, four years after the accident. To put this in its proper context, 19,759 people were killed by the earthquake and tsunami that caused the accident at the plant. Furthermore, a 2013 UNSCEAR report found that there have been no radiation-related fatalities or acute diseases among the local population exposed to radioactive material. Once more, though, the disaster has contributed to a general distrust of nuclear energy among the populations of the world. As scientist Chris Hohenemser and his team note in the 1977 article in Science, "Society seems content to strike a more moderate or uncertain balance with other technologies than with nuclear power."

The Dream of Fusion

Nuclear fission works by harnessing energy from the split atom. Some scientists have proposed nuclear fusion as an alternative, in which atoms are fused in reactions that release a huge amount of energy as a by-product.

Humanity has successfully created devices that utilize nuclear fusion in an uncontrolled manner; that is, thermonuclear, hydrogen bombs. Teller was working on the H-bomb as early as 1944, and the first thermonuclear explosion took place on November 1, 1952. The key is harnessing this technology in a controlled way, that can be used as a source of energy, rather than devastation. This has proven a more difficult scientific matter.

Nuclear fusion is how stars create their own energy. Hydrogen atoms are fused at high pressures and temperatures to form helium. However, as science reporter Justine Calma (2022) notes, it turns out that "It's really hard to recreate a star in a lab." A vast amount of temperature and pressure is needed to create the conditions for nuclear fusion, and this is very hard (and expensive) to produce safely. Scientists have realized that they can use lasers to create conditions for fusion, avoiding some of these difficulties, but plenty of work still needs to be done on refining the process and achieving a net-positive amount of energy.

On the other hand, the dream of nuclear fusion lives on in the research of physicists and technicians. Nuclear fusion has all the advantages of nuclear fission and more. Like fission, it does not produce harmful greenhouse gasses and is therefore a clean source of energy. Moreover, unlike fission, nuclear fusion does not produce radioactive waste. Instead, it produces helium—the same gas that we put in balloons. Perhaps best of all, if controlled nuclear fusion is achieved, the input material is hydrogen: "The simplest and most abundant element in the universe" (Calma, 2022). We can get hydrogen from seawater, and the United States Department of Energy estimates that fusion will be able to convert one gallon of seawater into as much energy as given by 300 gallons of gasoline (Lanctot, n.d.).

We are still some distance from achieving controlled nuclear fusion. However, there is encouraging progress being made. On December 5, 2022, scientists at the Lawrence Livermore National Lab achieved "fusion ignition," in which a net increase of energy was produced in a fusion reaction (Calma, 2022). Lasers shot 2.05 megajoules at their target to trigger a fusion reaction, which in turn produced 3.15 megajoules. This sounds promising, but it is also worth noting that the lasers themselves used up 300 megajoules from the grid, so there is still some way to go. Furthermore, for nuclear fusion plants to be commercially viable, a 1.5 megajoule net energy gain is insufficient. Calma (2022) estimates that "you'll need a gain of 50 to 100 instead."

Nonetheless, experiments like the one at Lawrence Livermore National Lab give us reasons to be optimistic. In a few decades, we may well have nuclear fusion plants, providing an abundance of clean energy for the world to use. Though it is unlikely that such developments will come in time to have a significant impact on the growing ecological disaster of climate change, such technologies may prove utterly revolutionary to global politics.

CONCLUSION

The history of nuclear technology is a fraught one. Its main characters were conflicted and complicated men, full of regrets, guilt, and passion. Oppenheimer was once the most celebrated scientist in the United States but died in relative obscurity after years of political persecution. Einstein was sidelined and regretful of his role in sending a letter to Roosevelt, even though the famous physicist was not involved in the Manhattan Project itself. Szilárd desperately tried to stop the bomb he helped create from being used, and failed. Petitions, public statements, reports... for all the efforts of those involved in the Manhattan Project, the bombs were dropped on Hiroshima and Nagasaki, the hydrogen bomb was soon developed, and the United States and Soviet Russia engaged in an arms race to gather stockpiles large enough to destroy the world several times over.

And yet, many of the scientists who later campaigned against nuclear proliferation and advocated for international control of nuclear weapons were the same people enthusiastically working on creating the atomic bomb. Oppenheimer aided the Target Committee and explained to the American Airforce at which height to detonate the atomic bomb to cause the most devastation. Bohr worked on the ignition device that made possible implosion-type atomic weapons. Even Szilárd—ever the moral contrarian and thorn in Groves's side—helped design the bomb, and helped advocate for the Manhattan Project in the letter to Roosevelt.

Whether or not the key individuals involved in the birth of the atomic age regretted their actions, then, is complicated. It is perhaps easier to judge from a position of distance and hindsight, but it must have been entirely baffling to these relatively young men of science. We know that the Nazi bomb project barely got off the ground, but can we blame Oppenheimer and Szilárd for worrying about atomic weapons in Hitler's hands?

Moreover, the more you learn about the history of the twentieth century, the less straightforward the moral questions become. Have nuclear weapons saved lives? Might the United States and the Soviet Union have waged direct war if not for nuclear weapons and the principle of mutually assured destruction? Would Imperial Japan have surrendered if the bomb had been demonstrated first, or would more American and Japanese lives have been lost for the sparing of Hiroshima and Nagasaki? Has the weaponization of nuclear power undone any chance of the proliferation of clean, nuclear energy?

Underlying these questions and speculations are then deeper, moral considerations. Should we judge the ethics of nuclear weapons simply by comparing the number of lives lost? Is this the correct moral way to approach the issue, or is there a more basic ethical line that was crossed simply by creating such devices? And then there is the million-dollar question: Will nuclear weapons be used again in the future? Will there come a time when humanity destroys itself through thermonuclear war? And, if that time comes, does it matter if the existence of nuclear weapons has saved lives in the meantime?

This book has not sought to answer these questions definitively. Instead, it has given you the tools to think about these difficult problems and reach your own conclusions. The only certainty is that these moral questions are difficult. Beware certainty or quick judgments. These are deep, intractable problems that humanity as a whole must grapple with, and anyone claiming to have an easy answer is probably selling you something.

By adopting a character-led narrative and focusing on the figures involved in the Manhattan Project, this book has tried to make the history of this difficult time more accessible and to bring you into the world that the men and women of this era were experiencing. You have read first-hand accounts of the spectacle of the Trinity test, the horror of Hiroshima and Nagasaki, and the reflections of the key individuals involved in these fateful decisions. Hopefully, you now not only have a greater understanding of the main facts, but you have an increased empathy for the decision-makers of the 1940s, 1950s, and beyond. Hopefully, you understand not only on a factual level but on an emotional level, as well.

The onus is now on you. If this topic continues to interest you—and we at History

Brought Alive hope that it does—continue to read on the subject and do your own research, gathering more and more data so you can reach your own conclusions. Read books, browse firsthand accounts from organizations like the Atomic Heritage Foundation, and embrace your curiosity. The history of the Manhattan Project continues to have a profound influence on the modern world. The relationships between Russia and NATO, the conflict between Pakistan and India, and the activities of North Korea: These are all issues that are fundamentally impacted by the existence of nuclear weapons. To understand the history of these matters is to better understand what is happening now, empowering you to make your own decisions, and to reflect on current politics about the world.

So, if we at History Brought Alive would like you to take away only one message from reading this book, it is this: Reflect on the insights it has provided. Think about the issues contained within. Recognize the importance of responsible use of technology, and apply that thinking to current issues about climate change, energy policy, and artificial intelligence. Continue to embrace your curiosity and need for understanding, and join the call for a more peaceful and informed future.

REFERENCES

Academic Accelerator. (n.d.). *German nuclear weapons program.* https://academic-accelerator.com/encyclopedia/german-nuclear-weapons-program

Aljazeera. (2023, March 25). *Russia's nuclear arsenal: How big is it and who controls it?* https://www.aljazeera.com/news/2023/3/25/russias-nuclear-arsenal-how-big-is-it-and-who-controls-it

American Museum of Natural History. (n.d.). *The great debate.* https://www.amnh.org/exhibitions/einstein/legacy/quantum-theory

Anderson, P. S. (2018, May 22). *Interview by N, Weisenberg.* Atomic Heritage Foundation https://ahf.nuclearmuseum.org/voices/oral-histories/philip-s-anderson-jrs-interview/

Arms Control Association. (2023, June). *Nuclear weapons: who has what at a glance.* https://www.armscontrol.org/factsheets/Nuclearweaponswhohaswhat

Atomic Heritage Foundation (n.d.a). *Edward Teller.* https://ahf.nuclearmuseum.org/ahf/profile/edward-teller/

Atomic Heritage Foundation. (n.d.b). *Enrico Fermi.* https://ahf.nuclearmuseum.org/ahf/profile/enrico-fermi/

Atomic Heritage Foundation. (n.d.c). *Leo Szilárd.* https://ahf.nuclearmuseum.org/ahf/profile/leo-Szilárd/

Atomic Heritage Foundation. (2016, July 15). *Leo Szilárd's fight to stop the bomb.* https://ahf.nuclearmuseum.org/ahf/history/leo-Szilárds-fight-stop-bomb/

Atomic Heritage Foundation. (2017, July 18). *The Einstein-Szilárd Letter – 1939.* https://ahf.nuclearmuseum.org/ahf/history/einstei

n-Szilárd-letter-1939/

Bethe, H. (2006, November 10 / 1954). *Testimony in the matter of J. Robert Oppenheimer*. Atomic Archives. https://www.atomicarchive.com/resources/docume nts/oppenheimer/trial-bethe.html

Beyler, R. (n.d.). *Heisenberg and the nazi party*. Britannica. https://www.britannica.com/biography/Werner-Heisenberg/Heisenberg-and-the-Nazi-Party

Bohr, N. (1950, June 9). *Open letter to the United Nations*. Atomic Archive. https://www.atomicarchive.com/resources/docume nts/deterrence/bohr-un-letter.html

Born, M., Bridgman, P. W., Einstein, A., Infeld, L., Joliot-Curie, F., Muller, H. J., Pauling, L., Powell, C. F., Rotblat, J., Russell, B. & Yukawa, H. (1955, July 9). *The Russell-Einstein manifesto*. Pugwash. https://pugwash.org/1955/07/09/statement-manifesto/

Boyd, A. (n.d.). *The Bohr-Einstein debates. The Engines of Our Ingenuity*. https://engines.egr.uh.edu/episode/2627

Burton, K. D. (n.d.). *Cold conflict*. The National WWII Museum. https://www.nationalww2museum.org/war/articles /cold-conflict

Calma, J. (2022, December 16). *What in the world is nuclear fusion—and when will we harness it?* The Verge. https://www.theverge.com/23508872/nuclear-fusion-power-clean-energy-breakthrough-explained

Close, F. (2019). *Trinity: The treachery and pursuit of the most dangerous spy in history*. Allen Lane.

Cooper, H., Gibbons-Neff, T., Schmitt, E. & Barnes, J. E. (2023, August 18). *Troop deaths and injuries in Ukraine War near 500,000, U.S. officials say*. The New York Times. https://www.nytimes.com/2023/08/18/us/politics/ ukraine-russia-war-casualties.html

Cramer, M. (2022, July 15). *'Now I am become death': The legacy of the first nuclear bomb test*. The New York Times. https://www.nytimes.com/2020/07/15/us/trinity-test-anniversary.html

Donne, J. (1896). *Poems of John Donne, volume 1*. Lawrence & Bullen.

Eckert, M. (2001, November 30). *Werner Heisenberg: controversial scientist*. Physics World. https://physicsworld.com/a/werner-heisenberg-controversial-scientist/

Einstein, A. (1905). Does the inertia of a body depend on its energy content? *Annalen der Physik, 17*(891).

Einstein, A. (1939, August 2). *Einstein's letter to President Roosevelt – 1939*. Atomic Archive. https://www.atomicarchive.com/resources/documents/beginnings/einstein.html

Farrell, T. F. & Groves, L. (n.d./1945, July 18). *Report on the Trinity test by General Groves - 1945*. Atomic Archive. https://www.atomicarchive.com/resources/documents/trinity/groves.html#

Fine, L. & Remington, J. A. (1972). *The corps of engineers: construction in the United States*. Washington, D.C.

Foulds, T. (2019, January 15). *Interview by D. Steele & T. Pritikin* [Transcript]. Atomic Heritage Foundation. https://ahf.nuclearmuseum.org/voices/oral-histories/tom-fouldss-interview/

Franck, J., Hughes, D. J., Nickson, J. J., Rabinowitch, E., Seaborg, G. T., Stearns, J. C. & Szilárd, L. (1945, June 11). *The Franck report*. Atomic Heritage Foundation. https://ahf.nuclearmuseum.org/ahf/key-documents/franck-report/

Frank, R. B. (1999). *Downfall: the end of the Imperial Japanese Empire*. New York: Random House.

Granholm, J. (2022, December 16). *Secretary Granholm's statement on DOE order vacating 1954 Atomic Energy Commission decision in the matter of*

J. Robert Oppenheimer. Energy.gov. https://www.energy.gov/articles/secretary-granholm-statement-doe-order-vacating-1954-atomic-energy-commission-decision

Groves, L. R. (1965a, January 5). *Interview by S. Groueff – Part 1* [Transcript]. Atomic Heritage Foundation. https://ahf.nuclearmuseum.org/voices/oral-histories/general-leslie-grovess-interview-part-1/

Groves, L. R. (1965b, January 6). *Interview by S. Groueff – Part 6* [Transcript]. Atomic Heritage Foundation. https://ahf.nuclearmuseum.org/voices/oral-histories/general-leslie-grovess-interview-part-6/

Groves, L. R. (1965c, January 8). *Interview by S. Groueff – Part 11* [Transcript]. Atomic Heritage Foundation. https://ahf.nuclearmuseum.org/voices/oral-histories/general-leslie-grovess-interview-part-11/

Groves, L. R. (1965d, June 20). *Interview by S. Groueff – Part 3* [Transcript]. Atomic Heritage Foundation. https://ahf.nuclearmuseum.org/voices/oral-histories/general-leslie-grovess-interview-part-3/

Harrington, K. (2023, July 25). *Oppenheimer: Who is Werner Heisenberg?* Dexerto. https://www.dexerto.com/tv-movies/oppenheimer-who-is-werner-heisenberg-2224270/

Herken, G. (2016, November 18). *He's the bomb: an Enrico Fermi biography*. New York Times. https://www.nytimes.com/2016/11/20/books/review/enrico-fermi-biography-pope-of-physics.html

Hirohito. (1945, August 15). *Hirohito surrender broadcast*. NHK.

History.com Editors. (2023, August 13). *The birth of quantum theory*. https://www.history.com/this-day-in-history/the-birth-of-quantum-theory

Hohenemser, C., Kasperson, R. & Kates, R. (1977). The distrust of nuclear power. *Science, 196*(4285), 25-34. doi: 10.1126/science.841337.

Holloway, D. (1994). *Stalin and the bomb*. Yale University Press.

Howes, R. H. & Herzenberg, C. L. (2003). *Their day in the*

sun: women of the Manhattan Project. Temple University Press.

Hoyt, E. P. (2001) *Japan's war: the Great Pacific conflict.* New York: McGraw-Hill

Isaacson, W. (2007). *Einstein: his life and universe.* Simon & Schuster.

Jahn, G. (1962). *Award ceremony speech* [Transcript]. Nobel Prize. https://www.nobelprize.org/prizes/peace/1962/ceremony-speech/

Jogalekar, A. (2014, January 15). *The many tragedies of Edward Teller.* Scientific American. https://blogs.scientificamerican.com/the-curious-wavefunction/the-many-tragedies-of-edward-teller/

Kapur, S. P. (2017). Stability-instability paradox. In F. M. Moghaddam (Ed.), *The SAGE Encyclopedia of Political Behavior.* SAGE Publications.

Krieger, D. (2008, January 13). *Ronald Reagan: a nuclear abolitionist.* Nuclear Age Peace Foundation. https://www.wagingpeace.org/ronald-reagan-a-nuclear-abolitionist/

Lanctot, M. (n.d.). *DOE explains... deuterium-tritium fusion reactor fuel.* Department of Energy. https://www.energy.gov/science/doe-explainsdeuterium-tritium-fusion-reactor-fuel

Lista, D. (2012, August 9). *Hiroshima and Nagasaki: the long term health effects.* Columbia K=1 Project. https://k1project.columbia.edu/news/hiroshima-and-nagasaki#

Macrakis, K. (1993). *Surviving the swastika: scientific research in Nazi Germany.* Oxford University Press.

Manjunath, R. (2021, May 13). *Letter from Heinrich Himmler to Werner Heisenberg.* LinkedIn. https://www.linkedin.com/pulse/letter-from-heinrich-himmler-werner-heisenberg-manjunath-r

McMillan, P. J. (1994, October 2). *Science and secrecy.* New York Times. https://archive.nytimes.com/www.nytimes.com/books/98/12/06/specials/holloway-stalin.html

Muon Ray, Teller, E. (2012, March 17). *Edward Teller on the Trinity nuclear bomb test* [Video]. YouTube. https://www.youtube.com/watch?v=zV2W5yepiA0&ab_channel=MuonRay

Nichols, K. D. (1954). *Findings and recommendations of the Personnel Security Board in the matter of Dr. J. Robert Oppenheimer.* Reprinted by the Avalon Project. https://avalon.law.yale.edu/20th_century/opp01.asp

Norris, R. S. (2022). *Racing for the bomb: General Leslie R. Groves, the Manhattan Project's indispensable man.* Steerforth Press.

Nova (n.d.). *Einstein's big idea.* PBS. https://www.pbs.org/wgbh/nova/einstein/lrk-hand-emc2expl.html#

Oi, M. (2015, August 9). *The man who saved Kyoto from the atomic bomb.* BBC News. https://www.bbc.co.uk/news/world-asia-33755182

Oppenheimer, J. R. (1965, September 12). *Interview by S. Groueff* [Transcript]. Atomic Heritage Foundation. https://ahf.nuclearmuseum.org/voices/oral-histories/j-robert-oppenheimers-interview/

Phillips, K. (2018, July 17). *'He is honest—but smart as hell': when Truman met Stalin.* The Washington Post. https://www.washingtonpost.com/news/retropolis/wp/2018/07/17/he-is-honest-but-smart-as-hell-when-truman-met-stalin/

Preston, D. L., Shimizu, Y., Pierce, D. A., Suyama, A. & Mabuchi, K. (2003). Studies of mortality of atomic bomb survivors. Report 13: solid cancer and noncancer disease mortality: 1950-1997. *Radiation Research 160*(4), 381-407.

Rauchhaus, R. (2009). Evaluating the nuclear peace hypothesis—a quantitative approach. *Journal of Conflict Resolution, 53*(2), 258-277.

Rhodes, R. (1986). *The making of the atomic bomb.* New York, NY: Simon & Schuster.

Rhodes, R. (2017). *Clashing colleagues.* UChicago Magazine. https://mag.uchicago.edu/science-medicine/clashing-colleagues#

Rozsa, M. (2023, August 2). *Oppenheimer's hero Niels Bohr has a legacy as complicated as the "father of the atomic bomb".* Salon. https://www.salon.com/2023/08/02/oppenheimers-hero-niels-bohr-has-a-legacy-as-complicated-as-the-father-of-the-atomic-bomb/

Russell, L. (2018, April 25). *Interview by N. Weisenberg* [Transcript]. Atomic Heritage Foundation. https://ahf.nuclearmuseum.org/voices/oral-histories/liane-russells-interview/

Schultz, G. P., Perry, W. J., Kissinger, H. A. & Nunn, S. (2007, January 4). *A world free of nuclear weapons.* The Wall Street Journal. https://www.nti.org/wp-content/uploads/2021/09/A-World-Free-of-Nuclear-Weapons.pdf

Sime, R. L. (2006, March). The politics of memory: Otto Hahn and the Third Reich. *Physics in Perspective, 8*(1), 3-51. doi:10.1007/s00016-004-0248-5

Sleight, J. (2019, July 25). *Scientists and the bomb: 'the destroyer of worlds'.* Global Zero. https://www.globalzero.org/updates/scientists-and-the-bomb-the-destroyer-of-worlds/

Spartacus Educational. (n.d.). *Fritz Strassman.* https://spartacus-educational.com/2WWstrassmann.htm

Speicher, J. (2023, July 27). *The true story behind Oppenheimer's communist connections.* Collider. https://collider.com/oppenheimer-communist-true-story/

Szilárd, L. (1945, July 17). *A petition to the President of the United States.* Reprinted by the Atomic Heritage Foundation. https://ahf.nuclearmuseum.org/ahf/key-documents/szilard-petition/

Szilárd, L. (1947). Letter to Stalin. *Bulletin of the Atomic Scientists 3*(12). 347-349.

https://doi.org/10.1080/00963402.1947.11459140

Target Committee. (n.d.). *Notes on initial meeting of Target Committee.* nsarchive. https://nsarchive2.gwu.edu/NSAEBB/NSAEBB162/4.pdf

Teller, E. (1986, September 12). *Interview by S. L. Sanger.* Voices of the Manhattan Project, Atomic Heritage Foundation. https://ahf.nuclearmuseum.org/voices/oral-histories/edward-tellers-interview/

The New York Times. (1967, February 19). *J. Robert Oppenheimer, atom bomb pioneer, dies. On this Day* [Archive]. https://archive.nytimes.com/www.nytimes.com/learning/general/onthisday/bday/0422.html

The Nobel Prize. (2023, August 11). *Enrico Fermi.* https://www.nobelprize.org/prizes/physics/1938/fermi/biographical/

The Nobel Prize. (2023, August 14). *Werner Heisenberg.* https://www.nobelprize.org/prizes/physics/1932/heisenberg/biographical/

Tomonaga, M. (2019, February 19). *Interview by C. Kelly* [Transcript]. Atomic Heritage Foundation. https://ahf.nuclearmuseum.org/voices/oral-histories/masao-tomonagas-interview/

Truman, H. S. (1945, August 6). *Statement by the President of the United States* [Transcript]. American Experience. https://www.pbs.org/wgbh/americanexperience/features/truman-hiroshima/

United Nations. (2023, March 31). *Risk of nuclear weapons use higher than any time since Cold War, disarmament affairs chief warns security council.* https://press.un.org/en/2023/sc15250.doc.htm

United States Holocaust Memorial Museum. (2019, October 18). *Kristallnacht.* Holocaust Encyclopedia. https://encyclopedia.ushmm.org/content/en/article/kristallnacht

UNSCEAR. (2013). Level and effects of radiation

exposure due to the nuclear accident after the 2011 great east-Japan earthquake and tsunami. *UNSCEAR 2013 Report, Vol I, Annex A.*

UNSCEAR & Balanov, M. (2011). Health effects due to radiation from the Chernobyl accident. *UNSCEAR 2008 Report, Vol II, Annex D.*

U.S. Department of Energy. (n.d.). *Einstein's letter.* The Manhattan Project: an interactive history. https://www.osti.gov/opennet/manhattan-project-history/Events/1939-1942/einstein_letter.htm

Vyasa. (2nd to 5th century BCE). *Bhagavad Gita.*

Wellerstein, A. (2015, May 11). *What did Bohr do at Los Alamos?* Restricted Data. https://blog.nuclearsecrecy.com/2015/05/11/bohr-at-los-alamos/

Wells, H. G. (1914). *The world set free: a story of mankind.* Macmillan & Co.

Wisconsin Project on Nuclear Arms Control. (n.d.). *Nuclear weapons primer.* https://www.wisconsinproject.org/nuclear-weapons/

World Nuclear Association. (2023, May). *Nuclear power in the world today.* https://world-nuclear.org/information-library/current-and-future-generation/nuclear-power-in-the-world-today.aspx#

Yachting.com. (2023, August 23). *Albert Einstein: the passionate sailor.* https://www.yachting.com/en-gb/news/albert-einstein-the-passionate-sailor

FREE BONUS FROM HBA: EBOOK BUNDLE

Greetings!

First of all, thank you for reading our books. As fellow passionate readers of History and Mythology, we aim to create the very best books for our readers.

Now, we invite you to join our VIP list. As a welcome gift, we offer the History & Mythology Ebook Bundle below for free. Plus, you can be the first to receive new books and exclusives! <u>Remember it's 100% free to join.</u>

Simply scan the QR code to join.

OTHER BOOKS BY
HISTORY BROUGHT ALIVE

Available now in Ebook, Paperback, Hardcover, and Audiobook in all regions.

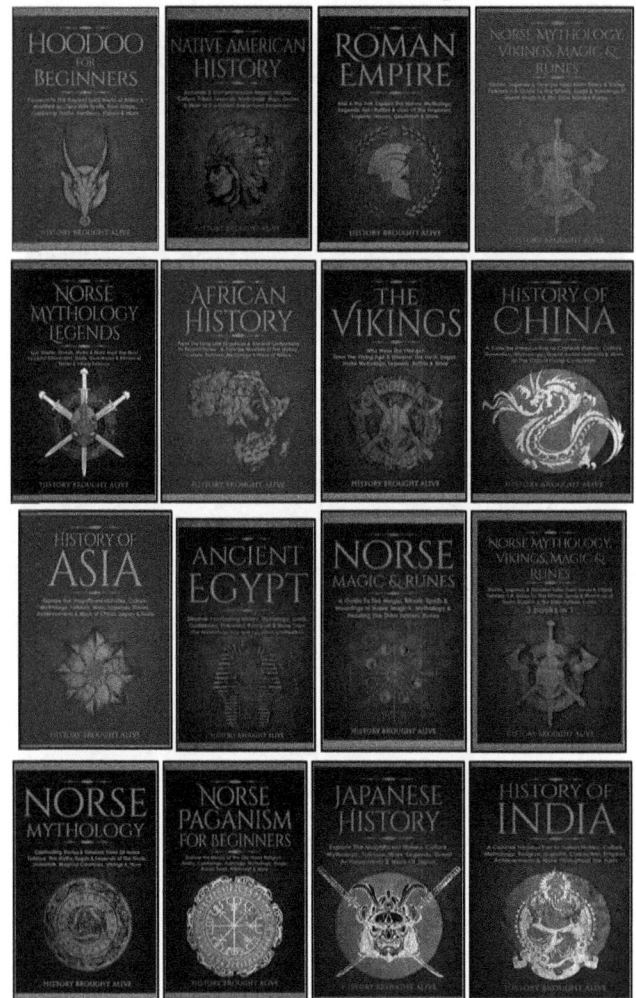

For Kids:

RECKONING OF POWER

We sincerely hope you enjoyed our new book ***"Reckoning of Power"***. We would greatly appreciate your feedback with an honest review at the place of purchase.

First and foremost, we are always looking to grow and improve as a team. It is reassuring to hear what works, as well as receive constructive feedback on what should improve. Second, starting out as an unknown author is exceedingly difficult, and Amazon reviews go a long way toward making the journey out of anonymity possible. Please take a few minutes to write an honest review.

Best regards,
History Brought Alive
http://historybroughtalive.com/

Milton Keynes UK
Ingram Content Group UK Ltd.
UKHW020934181023
430840UK00013B/421